CELTIC CONNECTIONS

CELTIC CONNECTIONS

The Ancient Celts, Their Tradition and
Living Legacy

EDITED BY DAVID JAMES

PHOTOGRAPHS BY SIMANT BOSTOCK

BLANDFORD

'To the many wondrous ancient and sacred sites of our planet, and to their guardians and protectors, both seen and unseen'

First published in the UK 1996 by Blandford
A Cassell Imprint
CASSELL PLC
Wellington House
125 Strand
London WC2R 0BB

Distributed in the United States by Sterling Publishing Co., Inc.
387 Park Avenue South, New York, NY 10016-8810

Distributed in Australia by Capricorn Link (Australia) Pty Ltd
2/13 Carrington Road, Castle Hill, NSW 2154

A Cataloguing-in-Publication Data entry for this title is available
from the British Library

ISBN 0-7137-2604-0

Typeset by Keystroke, Jacaranda Lodge, Wolverhampton
Printed and bound in Spain by Bookprint

Page 1: Iona Abbey, from the Well of Healing
Page 2: Glastonbury Tor: 'The Isle of Avalon'

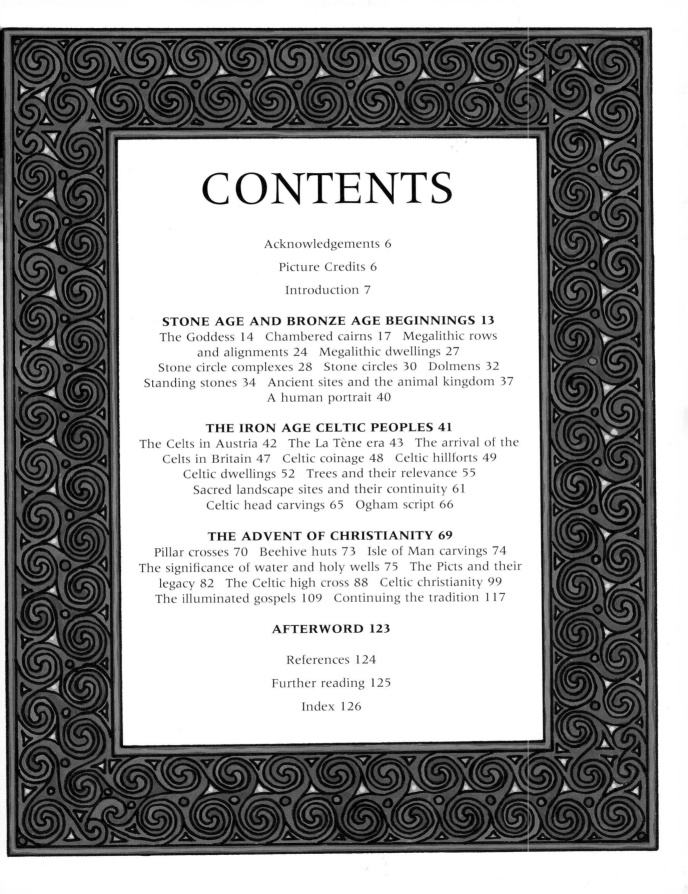

CONTENTS

ACKNOWLEDGEMENTS

Grateful thanks are extended to the following for permission to include their written contributions on the specific topics detailed below:

Simant Bostock Newgrange chambered cairn (p. 17); Carnac stone alignments (p. 24); Callanish stone circle complex (p. 28); Poulnabrone dolmen (p. 32). *Steve Dyer* Gavr'inis chambered cairn (p. 21). *Linda Todd* The Ring of Brodgar stone circle (p. 30). *Alan Pratt* Standing stones on North Uist (p. 35). *Dr Jutta Nordone* The Celts in Austria (p. 42). *Sarah King* The Celts in the Ardennes and the treasure of Vix (p. 46). *Frank James* Celtic coinage details (p. 48). *Paul Thomas* The Iron Age Celtic village at St Fagans, near Cardiff (p. 52). *Allen Meredith* Permission to reprint the information regarding his work with the Yew tree (p. 55). *Brian Lavelle* The Oak tree (pp. 59–60); Ogham script information (pp. 66, 68). *Jeffrey Samuel* Celtic head carving from Exmoor (p. 65). *Maureen Costain Richards* The Sandulf Cross, Isle of Man (p. 74). *James Gillon-Fergusson* Pictish carvings and miniatures (p. 82). *Geoff Pattison* The Sueno Stone (p. 85). *Marianna Lines* The Glamis Cross (p. 87). *Christopher Tweedale* The Isle of Islay and the Kildalton Cross (p. 90). *Claire Clancy* Muiredach's Cross, Monasterboice, Co. Louth, Ireland (p. 94). *Harold Costain Richards* The Lonan Cross, Isle of Man (p. 97). *Michael Howard* Celtic Christianity in Wales (p. 100). *Peter Glanville* Celtic Christianity in Iona (p. 104). *Mada James* St Aidan and Lindisfarne (p. 106). *Mike Davies* The Welsh lovespoon (p. 118). *George Stevens* The Irish harp (p. 119).

All other text and articles by David James, as copyright page details.

PICTURE CREDITS

Written consent has been obtained for all photographs and artwork except where noted.

All photographs are by Simant Bostock, with the exception of the following: p. 36 Alan Pratt, North Uist; p. 46 Sarah King, Luxemburg; p. 48 Dominic Wills, from the collection of S. W. Bragg; pp. 50, 51, 62, 63, 78, 93, 94 David James; pp. 7, 91 Christopher Tweedale; p. 96 Harold Costain Richards; p. 98 Arthur Pearse; pp. 107, 108, 109 Geoff Pattison; p. 113 reproduced with permission of the British Library, London (British Library MS folio 26b); pp. 117, 118 © Mike Davies Lovespoons, Newport, Gwent and reproduced with permission; p. 120 George Stevens; p. 122 by permission of Kora Wüthier, Rorschach, Switzerland; p. 86 © Paul Turner; p. 85 provided by a *Celtic Connections* subscriber but now untraceable; pp. 112, 114 Simon Rouse (1995).

Other illustrations: pp. 35, 67, 101, 103 Anthony Rees; pp. 74, 75 Maureen Costain Richards; pp. 82, 83, 84 James Gillon-Fergusson.

Painted Celtic knotwork borders by David James.

INTRODUCTION

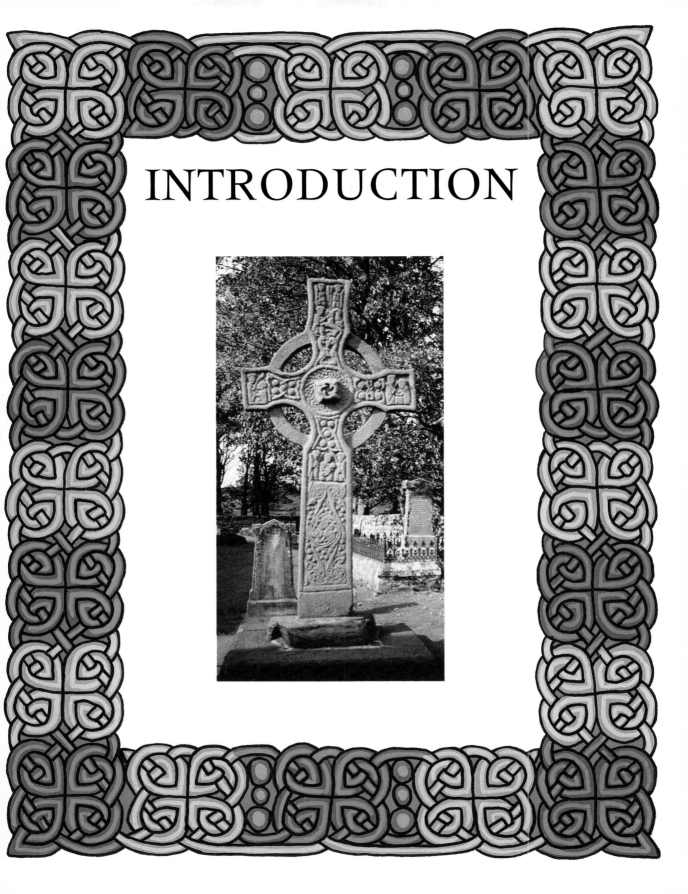

I HAVE had an interest, some people might call it an obsession, with the Celts for over 30 years. Like many of the good things that occur in our lives, there doesn't seem to be a rational explanation for this interest.

When I was 18 years old, I found myself very disillusioned with the options presented by conventional society, none of which provided me with an adequate means of creative expression at that time. In the summer of 1963, I travelled to Scotland with a very dear aunt, Jackie. We visited a wide area of the west coast, with which I felt an immediate affinity. After exploring the region around Oban, we camped in various remote locations on the Isle of Mull. The magnificent wide open spaces, with their mountains and lochs, seemed to resonate with something inside me; it was as though, in some way, I belonged there. In later years, when I became familiar with the concept of reincarnation, it certainly made me think that my love for western Scotland might well stem from having lived in that area in a previous life.

The reasons for this love of western Scotland, however, are un-important. The fact is that at an early age I became linked with the area, its unique and magical atmosphere, and, most important of all for me on that holiday, we made a day trip to the Isle of Iona.

This tiny little island, just five kilometres (three miles) long by two and a half kilometres (one and a half miles) wide, lies off the south-west tip of the Isle of Mull. I remember the day we visited the island very vividly. There was a Scotch mist hanging over it, and that very fine but penetrating drizzle, also frequently experienced in Ireland, which seems like nothing until you realize that your clothes are wet through. We had just one afternoon to see as much of the island as possible, and I remember taking off my damp shoes, rolling up my jeans and walking barefoot from the tiny jetty along the path to the abbey.

Due to the mist, many of the sights associated with the island were not visible, yet we passed and marvelled at St Martin's magnificent cross before entering the abbey buildings. Though the day was damp and grey, the atmosphere of the whole island, and of the abbey in particular, had the most profound effect on me.

At the age of 18 many of us tend not to rationalize events to any great degree, which for me, in hindsight, was a very good thing. Iona left me with the feeling that I wanted to return, and would do all that I could to make this happen.

Even after going back to the south of England, Iona was still very firmly in my mind. I had bought a few booklets about the island from the shop in the abbey precincts, and in one of them came across the name of Dr George MacLeod, the founder and organizer of the Iona Community at that time.

I wrote to the address given in the booklet, saying how much I was attracted to the island and asking if there would ever be a chance for me to work there in some capacity. Having very few qualifications and being only in my teens, I expected him to see this as just another letter from an enthusiastic young dreamer endeavouring to escape from the 'real world'. I was therefore extremely surprised to receive a letter by return post with an intriguing message: 'I'll be in London next week. Meet me for morning coffee in the Ritz if you'd like to.' This was followed by a date and a time.

I felt I had to go, although places like the Ritz were definitely not part of my daily life! Having arrived at the appointed time, I was greeted by this large, beaming minister who at once made me feel at ease. Our entire conversation lasted less than ten minutes, and I smile when I think back to it.

'Why do you want to work on the island?'

'Well, I don't really know, I'm just drawn to it.'

'Good . . . good. Do you have any family commitments?'

'No, I've just finished my studies and I'd like to live and work somewhere very remote.'

'Good . . . good. How do you fancy a winter on the island?'

I said that I'd like to give it a try.

'Fine, see you in Edinburgh in a week's time, and we'll go across from there. You'll have to excuse me now as I have another appointment.'

I was left with a warm glow inside and the sight of this large, genial man striding away down a crowded London street, his black cassock flapping in the breeze.

Needless to say, I accepted the opportunity and just over a week later found myself back on Iona, working for my keep, sharing in the many interesting jobs which are part of the daily routine of an island life.

It was at this point that my interest in the Celts really started. During the winter months, the afternoons were 'free time', and I was able to spend many of them in the abbey library. There I was able to discover, through various ancient books, much about the history and legends of the island, and, more than that, some of the history and legends of the Celts themselves and their known origins in Europe and even further afield.

The books which fascinated me the most were a couple of very early ones with steel engravings of Celtic crosses and ancient carvings from both western Scotland and Ireland. It was at this time that I became aware of the vast wealth of wondrous art in the form of illuminated manuscripts, stone carvings, high crosses and metalwork artefacts which had been created in all the Celtic countries many centuries ago.

The Iona crosses were beautifully depicted in one of these books, and it is with amusement that I look back on my first sketches of these magnificent sculptures. I had the idea that I would borrow a very soft pencil from someone on the island (which was no problem) and trace the outlines of these crosses from the books very carefully, using tracing paper. The latter, however, *did* prove a problem, as no one I talked to on the island had any, or anything like it, and the nearest possible source was Oban, one island and two ferry journeys away. So I followed the practical ways of the local inhabitants, who make good use of what is readily available (or happens to be washed ashore in a rough sea). What *was* readily available, as it was imported in bulk from the mainland, was Bronco toilet paper, and this proved excellent for the purpose of tracing the crosses. (Fortunately, this was before the days of the golden Labrador puppy promoting 'soft and long and strong', which is completely opaque and would therefore have been useless for my purpose.) I still have a couple of Bronco tracings of St John's cross on Iona, kept for sentimental reasons more than anything else.

While on Iona that winter, one job was assigned to me that was a particular joy; relabelling the stone carvings in the Abbey Museum, as the old labels had become almost illegible due to the damp, salt-laden atmosphere. Armed with a quantity of plain white postcards and a waterproof pen, I spent an entire fortnight working in the museum, taking with me sketch pad and pencil as well. To be in the vicinity of these wonderful ancient Celtic sculptures (not to mention a couple of equally beautiful and intricate eleventh-century Norse slab carvings) was an experience I shall never forget, and it certainly stimulated my enthusiasm for anything and everything to do with the Celts.

Eventually I returned to the south of England, but having lived in Scotland I now felt a bit like a fish out of water and eventually ended up moving to a remote area of south Wales, in the hills near Lampeter. Having developed a strong interest in all things Celtic, and also pre-historic sites such as chambered cairns, dolmens, and stone circles, this was an ideal place. With friends I visited many sites in the area, such

Mull of Kintyre and coast of Ireland from author's farmhouse

as the magnificent St Davids Cathedral, Pentre Ifan burial chamber, Nevern church with its great cross and ogham carvings, and St Non's sixth-century Celtic chapel set within a stone circle.

After this time in Wales, I stayed at the Findhorn Community in Morayshire, eastern Scotland, in the early 1970s. While there I was able to visit various Pictish sites and carvings, and experience firsthand some of the wonders and intricacies of these unique sculptures in stone.

Scotland's magnetic attraction prevailed again in the mid-1970s, when I moved to the Kintyre peninsula, living in a dilapidated Scottish farmhouse in the hills about six kilometres (four miles) from Campbeltown. This location afforded a great opportunity to visit, photograph and sketch many ancient sites, caves, Celtic chapels, crosses and carvings on Scotland's west coast, especially in the more remote areas.

Four years later I moved back to the south of England for family reasons, but continued creating Celtic paintings, writing articles for magazines and reading anything I could get hold of about the different Celtic countries, their early inhabitants and their culture.

It was during this time that I first met Simant Bostock, whose fine photographs illustrate this book. I had seen several very striking examples of his pictures of early Celtic sites in a national magazine and decided to write to him, introducing myself and my interests, and to express appreciation of his work. We met up in the summer of 1985, and I recall with amusement that he had brought with him ten photograph albums. When I expressed my surprise, he grinned and said, 'That's just to start with; there's plenty more!'

Since that time, we have worked together on a number of projects connected with Celtic and earlier sites, using his extensive library of pictures which range from Barra to Brittany, from Iona to remotest Ireland. For me he is one of those rare photographers who is able to capture the spirit and magic of an ancient place on film, whether by patiently waiting until the light is just right or by finding a very unusual view of it, or a combination of both, and more. His recent appearance on BBC television certainly did justice to his remarkable photographs of Glastonbury and the surrounding area.

In 1990 I moved to a very small chalet-type building overlooking the sea, in a remote part of Dorset, close to the Chesil Beach and lived here for over four years. With minimal electricity, no running water (there was a standpipe about 180 metres (600 ft) down the hill) and a wood-burning stove, this was an ideal place to start writing about my Celtic experiences. The format of my first book, *The Celtic Image*, created in conjunction with the Celtic artist Courtney Davis (who had also moved to the same part of the world) and subsequently published as a Blandford title by Cassell, was drafted here.

It was at this time that I placed a small advertisement in the Welsh Tourist Board publication *Newyddion Celtica* (*Celtica News*), saying that if there were folk keen on discovering more about Celtic subjects, I would be happy to correspond with them and share my knowledge, and, if I couldn't help, almost certainly I would 'know a man (or often woman) who could'.

I had expected just a few letters, so was completely amazed by the response. Enthusiasts were writing to me from as far afield as Russia, China, Brazil and Norway, to name but a few countries. As the mail built up, a very close friend, appropriately named Grace, had the inspired idea that I should start a small magazine containing information on Celtic subjects. She suggested that the name could be *Celtic Connections*, as it would serve to link Celtic-minded people everywhere. Without her enthusiasm and encouragement at that point, I don't think the magazine would have got off the ground, and I shall always be immensely grateful to her. She has inspired many people with different ventures and almost all of them have been successful, due to her very astute mind.

I'd never imagined editing a magazine, but the more I thought about it, the more it seemed a logical progression from all the correspondence that I was now engaged in. So, in 1992, *Celtic Connections* was born, and thanks to *Newyddion Celtica*, it received favourable promotion. For the last three years, the magazine has gone from strength to strength, and we now have subscribers worldwide. This book is based on some of the articles we have received, with additional text by myself, and is illustrated with Simant Bostock's beautiful and evocative photographs. Rather than a scholarly and long-winded treatise, it is intended as a lively introduction, both written and visual, to the intriguing and magical world of the Celts, from their earliest known times to the present day.

David James
Portesham, Dorset, UK

STONE AGE
AND
BRONZE AGE
BEGINNINGS

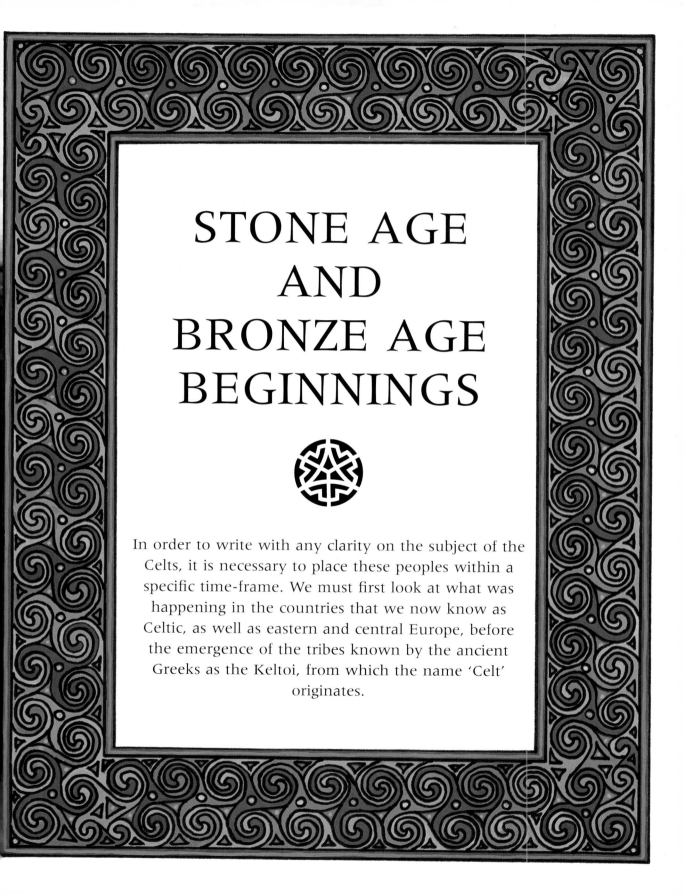

In order to write with any clarity on the subject of the
Celts, it is necessary to place these peoples within a
specific time-frame. We must first look at what was
happening in the countries that we now know as
Celtic, as well as eastern and central Europe, before
the emergence of the tribes known by the ancient
Greeks as the Keltoi, from which the name 'Celt'
originates.

THE GODDESS

A belief system which was continuous from the Late Palaeolithic era, *c.* 30,000 BC, right through to the advent of Christianity was the worship of the Goddess. This was a central theme throughout the Near East and Europe, and subsequently in Britain. As well as being the 'Giver of Birth', the Goddess symbolized the qualities or spirit of abundance, fertility and generosity inherent in the human, animal, plant and mineral kingdoms of the earth. Hence the phrase 'Mother Earth', which is still used today.

The Goddess was very much a part of the belief system of the Celts, whose presence in eastern and central Europe begins historically around 750 BC, although Celtic tribes had certainly been in existence for a considerable time before this.

The temple of Artemis at Ephesus in Turkey was one of the largest centres of Goddess worship during the first millennium BC. Votive offerings from many distant parts of Europe, as well as Egypt and the Near East, often in the form of small Goddess statues, have been discovered around the temple ruins, indicating that this was one of the major sites of pilgrimage. It should be remembered that the Celts were no strangers to this region, having crossed into Asia Minor in 267 BC, where some settled and were later said to have become 'the foolish Galatians' referred to in St Paul's letters.[1]

The worship of the Goddess was seen by the early Christians as incompatible with their own beliefs and so was denounced as heresy. Churches replaced the fine temples and today at some of the old ruins small Christian crosses can be found carved on the massive portals. This period marks the beginning of the male deity. It is strange to think that this masculine deity has been prevalent for only the last 2000 years. Prior to this, the Goddess had been venerated for almost 30,000 years.

This act of 'Christianizing' stones was widespread, and various standing stones, as well as stones with ogham inscriptions in Britain and Ireland, were given the same treatment, having small crosses carved on them.

For at least the first millennium BC the Goddess was venerated in Britain as Brigit or Bride; much later she became St Bride in the Christian hagiography. Her name means the Shining One. The origins of Brigit are Irish; her Brythonic counterpart was Arianrhod, the goddess associated with the full moon. Brigit was known as the Triple Goddess, symbolizing the three stages of maiden, mother and crone, and various small effigies have been discovered in this form. Not long ago a Triple Goddess sculpture was excavated at Minster Well, on the Isle of Sheppey in Kent. Her primary roles were as goddess of fertility, healing, arts and crafts and also poetry. Brigit or Bride must have been a figure of great importance, as her name was incorporated into a number of place-names, not least the Hebrides, off the western coast of Scotland.

Returning to the Goddess, the earliest known depiction of her is the Venus of Willendorf, a small limestone carving from Lower Austria with emphasized breasts and belly, short legs and tightly curled hair. Archaeologists date her to *c.* 30,000 BC.

During the Palaeolithic era caves were of great importance to our ancestors, the hunter-gatherers who roamed the earth. Many of the existing Goddess carvings were discovered in dark and spacious caves, whose walls were often covered with beautiful paintings of animals, birds and stylized humans. Some of the latter may well have been depictions of the Goddess herself. It seems likely that the cave represented the womb of Mother Earth, hence the direct link with the Goddess. The Goddess carving illustrated on page 16 is the Venus of Lespugue, who dates from *c.* 23,000 BC. She was found at the entrance to a cave in the Haute Garonne region of France.

The Venus of Willendorf (facsimile sculpture by Simant Bostock)

The Venus of Lespugue (facsimile sculpture by Simant Bostock)

We now continue from the start of the Mesolithic era, *c.* 10,000 BC, to the Neolithic or New Stone Age, *c.* 5000 to 2200 BC. This latter period saw the beginnings of agriculture, settled small communities, domestic animals, pottery-making and weaving. One of the main reasons for the establishment of these settled communities was a beneficial change in the climate.

Numerous small Goddess figures have been found from this period, illustrating a continuation of the old beliefs. Notable examples are the Lady of Pazardzik, from central Bulgaria, a carving that has been dated *c.* 4500 BC, and, slightly later, the Carnac Goddess from Brittany, with an emphasized vulva symbolizing the 'Giver of Birth'. The Carnac Goddess dates from 3500 BC.

CHAMBERED CAIRNS

It is during the Neolithic era that we can see the beginnings of the megalithic monuments, the best known of which are the chambered cairns or tombs. The word 'megalith' means large stone literally. From *c.* 4500 BC, and for a period of about 2000 years, these massive constructions were being built, coincident with the early clearing of the land and the first farming and agricultural settlements. The area in which these chambered cairns were constructed was more extensive than is often imagined, and included coastal regions of southern and western Spain, Corsica and Sardinia, northern Italy and most parts of France, and also western Britain, including Cornwall, Wales, Scotland and Ireland, as well as Germany, Denmark and southern Sweden.

These megalithic monuments were used for sacred purposes and can be seen as an integral part of the Goddess/Earth Mother tradition. The construction of many of them is highly sophisticated, with the passages to the inner chambers often aligned precisely with the rising sun at the winter solstice. The rays of the sun symbolically fertilized Mother Earth on this date, shining down the narrow passage and illuminating the inner chamber, which had been in darkness for the rest of the year. In this manner, the fertility of humans, animals and crops was believed to be ensured.

There are a number of magnificent examples of chambered cairns constructed during this period – for example, Maes Howe on the Orkney Isles and Bryn Celli Dhu on Anglesey. The two we will describe here, however, are Newgrange, in County Meath, Ireland, and Gavr'inis in the Golfe du Morbihan, Brittany. They contain some of the finest Neolithic stone carvings to be found anywhere. This impression of Newgrange by Simant Bostock was written after a recent visit to the site and the surrounding area.

> Newgrange – the enchanted palace; Brug Oengusa – the mansion of Oengus; Brug Maic Ind Óc – the home of the youthful hero; Sid in Bruca – the entrance to the Otherworld; Brú na Boinne – the house of the Boyne; the palace of the Gods. These are some of the many names that Newgrange has been called throughout the 5000 years of

its existence, a reminder of its association with the gods and goddesses of ancient Ireland.

Newgrange must certainly rate as one of the best megalithic monuments in Europe. Built *c.* 3200 BC, it predates Stonehenge and the pyramids in Egypt by several hundred years. Its huge, circular mound, 105 metres (340 ft) in diameter and 12 metres (40 ft) high, stands on top of the gently rising hills above the River Boyne in County Meath, Ireland. A façade of white quartz covers the south-eastern side, surrounding the entrance to the 18-metre-long (60 ft) passage that penetrates the interior and leads to the inner chamber at the heart of the mound. Giant kerbstones, 97 in all, many engraved with the finest examples of Neolithic art in existence – spirals, lozenges, zigzags and circles – edge the foot of the mound, and a huge blocking stone rests at the entrance. A stone circle, once containing 39 megaliths, 12 of which now remain, surrounds the monument. To the unsuspecting visitor, used to the overgrown ruins of many mega-lithic sites, Newgrange is quite a shock. Even for those familiar with the controversial reconstruction work undertaken by Michael O'Kelly, the archaeologist who excavated Newgrange between 1962 and 1975, the first sight of the monument can be awe-inspiring. It stands like a giant flying saucer that has just landed from outer space, its shining face of white quartz looking out in majestic silence over the green slopes of the Boyne valley; it is truly a place of the gods.

The River Boyne plays hostess to numerous other Neolithic monuments in this sacred landscape. Curving to the south to form the well-known bend in the Boyne, the river cradles two other enormous mounds, both visible from Newgrange. Upstream to the west, and promising to be equally spectacular, is Knowth, still undergoing exca-vation and reconstruction, with two passages, numerous engravings and 18 satellite mounds. To the east, downstream, Dowth, yet another

Exterior of Newgrange chambered cairn

enormous chambered cairn with two passages, lies overgrown and mysterious, awaiting excavation.

As with other megalithic sites, very little is known about the people who built these huge monuments. All that remained of these people at Newgrange were four huge, shallow stone basins on the floor of the alcoves of the inner chamber, some cremated human remains, bone beads and pins damaged from funeral pyres, stone pendants and seven stone balls, fragments of flint tools, animal bones and shells (the remains of ritual feasts, offerings to the spirits or nourishment for the dead), together with the unburnt remains of two people, and a pointed 'phallic' stone found outside the entrance. Stag and elk antlers were also reported to have been found when Newgrange was first opened in 1699.

The Neolithic people who built Newgrange seem to have belonged to a rich and powerful culture, farming and trading along the Atlantic coastline from the Orkneys to Brittany and beyond. Their great mega- lithic temples or ancestral shrines formed the spiritual centre of their communities and displayed the wealth and power of their kingdom or tribal territory. There the important members of the community were kept and honoured, perhaps kings or chieftains, priests or shamans, or others selected to represent the spirit of the people. There also the Great Goddess, Mother Earth, the sun and the rivers that made their land fertile were worshipped.

That Newgrange featured in some kind of midwinter religious festival of rebirth seems certain, constructed as it is so that on the winter solstice the rays of the rising sun shine through a small opening above the entrance and down the long passage into the darkness of the chamber deep within the mound. The thin beam of light illuminates the engraved megaliths and the remains of the ancestors interred within the womb-like cave of the Great Mother, fertilizing the land with the spirit of new life. It is hard to imagine a more symbolic repre- sentation of death and rebirth. The very architecture of the monument, with its 'text' of engraved symbols, the ancestral remains, the rising sun and the river all create a spectacular dramatic performance re-enacting the story of creation and the rebirth of the light. Paramount to the spirit of these people must have been the care of Mother Earth; the people were to live in harmony with her changing seasons and to ensure her continual fertility through magic and ritual.

According to Irish legend, the builders of Newgrange were the Tuatha Dé Danann – the people of the goddess Dana – a race of super- natural beings who originally came from the sky; a beautiful and magical people with heroic leaders and powerful magicians, half-gods half-men, invisible yet with the ability to assume human or animal form at will. For the Celts, 3000 years later, they became the Sidhe, the Shining Ones, Lords of Light, the Gentry or the fairy people who dwelt in the ancient mounds and forts guarding the entrance to the Otherworld of eternal youth and never-ending joy. Newgrange was the palace of Elcmar, the sky god, who was married to Boand, goddess of the River Boyne and the source of all wisdom and occult knowledge. By use of magic through which he masters time, Dagda, the all-knowing god of the sun and supreme chief of the Tuatha Dé Danann, took the palace from Elcmar and married Boand. From their union, Oengus was born, god of love and daylight, who eventually tricked his father into allowing him to reside at the palace of the Boyne for ever. The goddess Boand is also associated with the Celtic goddess Brigit and the later Christian saint Bride.

Newgrange's neighbouring mounds have their own mythology. Knowth – Cnogba – is connected with Englec, daughter of Elcmar and lover of Oengus, and is associated with the moon and the equinoxes. Dowth – Dubad – means darkness and is associated with winter solstice sunset and the longest night of the year. These ancient legends may reveal a great deal about the beliefs of the people who built and used Newgrange, as well as the spiritual beliefs of our Neolithic ancestors in general.

Entrance to Newgrange, showing carved portal and winter solstice aperture

Newgrange was for them the temple or palace of the living gods. From there the sun was born each year and magical re-enactments of the lives of their gods and heroes were probably performed by the shamans or priests. The patterns engraved on the kerbstones would have been part of this magic, symbolic of the eternal cycles of life, death and rebirth, the path of the spirit, the journey of the sun and the river of life, as well as the story of the mythical ancestors who created their land and their people.

For the Celts the Tuatha Dé Danann and the spirits of the natural world formed a major part of their spiritual beliefs. Offerings of gold torc, jewellery and coins were buried at Newgrange as late as the fourth century AD. The kings of Tara are said to have been buried there, together with 'three times 50 sons of kings', and their heroes were taken to the Otherworld by the Sidhe. In the Fennian cycle of tales, the love story of Dermaid and Grainne tells how Grainne, betrothed to Fion, the great war hero unsurpassed in wisdom and strength, falls in love with Dermaid, who is eventually killed by Fion. Oengus orders that the dead hero be lifted by the horsemen of the fairy mound to the house of the Boyne and the Otherworld. 'Since I cannot restore him to life,' says Oengus, 'I will send a soul into him so that he may talk to me each day.' At Newgrange, therefore, Oengus could reanimate the dead so that they spoke and performed the role of oracle.

Belief in the Sidhe or the fairy folk was so strong that even the Christian authorities could not deny their existence, but simply forbade the people to worship them. They were still seen at Newgrange by country folk well into this century. 'When they disappear, they go like fog. They must be something like spirits or how could they disappear in that way? I know of people who would milk in the fields about here and spill milk on the ground for the good people; and pots of potatoes would be put out for the good people at night.'[2] Others described the Sidhe as 'shining with an eerie light, some small and some very tall in stature'. It was felt that they still held power unseen as guardians of the land, and the health and fertility of the animals and crops depended upon their cooperation.

There is only one other chambered cairn with Neolithic artistic ornamentation in the form of stone carvings to rival Newgrange, and that is Gavr'inis, situated on an island in the Golfe du Morbihan in Brittany. This chambered cairn is of a similar date to Newgrange, and of the 29 great slabs which form the passage walls, 23 are profusely decorated. Here follows Steve Dyer's present-day description of this island site:

Gavr'inis has to be rated one of the finest prehistoric constructions in northern Europe. It also has to be one of the most attractive locations, sited as it is on a small island at the entrance to the Golfe du Morbihan in the south of Brittany. It is reckoned by conventional archaeological dating to be from *c.* 3500 BC. It is a raised cairn constructed of large blocks of stone piled up in a stepped pattern, and today has the appearance of a squat pyramid. The external appearance has though been both naturally eroded and reconstructed by various investigations in the past.

The scale of the construction is vast in proportion to the tunnel and chamber which reside within it. The entrance to the chamber appears almost ludicrously small in comparison to the huge bulk of the cairn itself. However, Gavr'inis is justly famous for another reason – its spectacularly carved stones which line the passageway and rear chamber. In northern Europe there is nothing to compare with the scale, detail or quantity of such patterns.

Gavr'inis is accessible only by boat from the nearby village of Lamor Baden. It is now an island, although geologically it was most likely connected by a continuous landmass with the neighbouring structures of Carnac and Locmariequer when first completed. It is now regrettably tailored into a slick tourist enterprise, complete with ushering guides. However, when we visited it in the spring, we were able to slip away from the official tour and gather the flavour of the site without modern interpretation. This was made more possible by the fact that the tour guide spoke only French, so we were free to see our own truth in the nature of the carvings. It was clear, however, by the guide's gestures and the odd French word that we knew, that great assumption had been cast into the realm of fact in order to satisfy the rational demands of the tourists.

The entrance to Gavr'inis is lined with massive stone blocks in contrast to the much smaller stones that pile up to form the cairn. The tunnel is approximately one and a half metres (five ft) high, so most people of average height have to stoop a little to get in. The width of the

Gavr'inis chambered cairn

tunnel is wider than one would expect, to allow the passage of just one person at a time. On entering the tunnel you are aware of being encased in massive blocks on all sides. They are laid on the passage floor, to the sides and above you. The passage is between nine and 12 metres (30 and 40 ft) long, but just four or five stones make up this wall. Their width and stature would, it seems, have been chosen for the sheer volume of space that they offer up to the artist or artists who carved them. Visually, in the dim glow of the fluorescent light mounted above, you are immediately struck by the dynamism and scale of the carvings right from the very first entrance stone.

Carved stones lining interior passage of Gavr'inis

They are clear and deep, though they are now in places far easier to see by the addition of smoke deposits which antiquarians and early visitors have laid down on the stones over time. There is little or no space on each stone left uncarved with beautiful and varied patterns. These seem to fall roughly into five classes, though no real conclusions can be drawn from this. There are what we may call 'radiants', 'half-circle' (rainbow), 'herringbone', 'dagger' and 'serpent' shapes. Each stone is uniquely endowed and seems to focus on a particular theme, inasmuch as some seem to be covered with nothing but interlacing 'rainbow' shapes and others with cutting 'dagger' and 'herringbone' shapes.

To us, though, they defied intellectual interpretation and more strongly seemed to celebrate the shape and structure of the stones themselves. Lines flow and curve to follow natural keylines in the stones and then appear to pick up a theme and go wild with artistic tangents.

The passageway leads to a large rear chamber, again flanked by massive blocks standing wide and tall. The carvings continue around the chamber, with one stone in particular standing out from the others. On the west side of the chamber this stone exhibits 'pockets'. These deep pockets recess into the stone in the form of three holes, but each open to the other to form a continuous recess behind them. The holes and space are plenty large enough for a hand to reach into. Their purpose is once again a mystery. Undoubtedly they have been used for centuries to hold candles for lighting the darkness within, yet nobody can be sure that this was their original purpose.

The experience of Gavr'inis is similar to any exposure to explosive creativity, infusing satisfaction and pleasure in what you are seeing. Yet the experience is made more intense by the awesome structure and age of the gallery. One is left with the impression that for whatever reason or purpose, Gavr'inis was constructed by people who were intent on celebrating and exploring the constructs and patterns of nature, possibly for no other reason than that they found them profound and intrinsically pleasing. It remains, over 5000 years on, a place of affinity and inspiration for the twentieth-century soul.

MEGALITHIC ROWS AND ALIGNMENTS

Also in Brittany, not far from Gavr'inis, are the famous stone alignments at Carnac. For sheer quantity, this area is the greatest centre of megaliths in the world, and the monuments cover a period from 4700 BC (the earliest radiocarbon date, from a stone chamber at Kercado) to well after 2000 BC. They range from dolmens and massive menhirs or single standing stones to very large cairns, man-made mounds, and the vast alignments of standing stones which cover several square kilometres of the Breton countryside.

To find out more about this extraordinary site we have this description by Simant Bostock of a visit to the area:

The area around Carnac in Brittany contains not only one of the highest concentrations of megalithic sites anywhere in the world but also some of the most extraordinary.

The stone rows or alignments of standing stones are the best known and the most mysterious. Three main groups of alignments at Kerlescan, Kermario and Menec comprised over 3000 remaining megaliths, run for nearly five kilometres (three miles) through gorse and bracken, pine woods and worn sandy ground, each group of several parallel lines of stones ending in a giant enclosure. Rising from the mist the ancient stones of Carnac make their way across the land, a procession of grey figures moving slowly and endlessly westwards, towards the home of the setting sun. They mark the path of the spirit of a people who came to settle on the edge of the western ocean: dwellers of the threshold, guardians of the entrance to the Otherworld.

For more than 6000 years the megalithic monuments of western Europe have inspired the imagination. The Neolithic and Bronze Age cultures that built them flourished along the Atlantic coastline for 3000 years, leaving a legacy of a variety of ceremonial monuments – giant menhirs and dolmens, avenues and circles, cairns, passages and chambers. The Celtic tribes that succeeded them honoured the sanctity and magical power of these places. They were the home of the Shining Ones, the good people, the fairy folk, the Tuatha Dé Danann or the People of the Goddess. These beings had made an agreement with the warrior Celts to retreat into the hollow hills, the ancient

Stone alignments at Carnac

shrines and secret places of the earth, to live for ever in the Otherworld on condition that the sacred land and all life upon it was honoured and treated with respect. Many of the names of the megalithic monuments bear testimony to their being the domain of the fairies – the Rock of the Fairies, the House of the Witches, the House of the Dwarfs, etc.

In silence the stones have watched the years passing; millennia after millennia of different peoples and changing ways; honoured and worshipped by some, feared and desecrated by others. As one writer put it, 'Although the stones have remained silent, scholars have been loquacious on their behalf.' Thus they have been tenuously linked with pagan worship, tribal gatherings and tribal dancing, sacred avenues for religious processions and festivals, fertility rites and magic rituals, healing, witchcraft, sacrifice, memorials to the dead, a great battle, Atlantis, a matriarchal golden age of peace and harmony, a warrior slave society with a powerful ruling élite, the Great Goddess, gods, ancestors, fairies, giants, druids, petrified sinners, extraterrestrials, geomancy, earth energy, ley lines, sacred geometry, astronomy and more!

The ancient stones have long been seen as human figures or spirits of the gods or ancestors that can on occasions move or communicate with the living. They stand like modern sculptures in a landscape constructed for vast numbers of people to visit as a place of pilgrimage. The passages and chambers of the cairns and dolmens are symbolic of the womb of the Great Goddess, fecundated by the power of the sun, whose light penetrates the darkness once a year, often at the time of the winter solstice. Thus they may have received the spirits of the dead for resurrection and rebirth; and acted as shrines and temples where the spirits of the ancestors were honoured and could be contacted.

In Brittany well into the twentieth century the stones were associated with the spirits of the dead and the Otherworld by local peasants: 'We believe that the spirits of the ancestors surround us and live with us.'[3] The Ankou, or Lord of the Dead, was frequently heard driving his death cart among the stones, collecting the souls of the dead. The names of the alignments – Kerlescan, the house of burning, and Kermario, the house of the dead – could well refer to ancient funeral rites.

A local legend tells of Carnac's patron saint, Cornely, protector of cattle and horned animals, who, fleeing from the invading Romans with his two oxen, turned the pursuing army into stone. Cattle are still blessed during a festival at the local church and the association with cattle could well arise from memories of an ancient bull cult, or the ancient Celtic festivals when cattle – the principal source of wealth and symbol of fertility – were blessed by being driven through the Beltane fires into the ancient enclosures. Many of the megaliths have been associated with fertility, and folk customs involving women rubbing their bodies against the stones and couples making love among them to ensure a healthy pregnancy are well attested.

The original purpose of the megaliths and the spiritual beliefs of our ancestors may be lost to us for ever, yet the stones continue to draw us and remain a continual source of wonder and inspiration. The ancient stones of Carnac, whatever else they may be, are a memorial to the enduring spirit of a people, a legacy from our ancestors, reaching out to us from the past to share their destiny with us.

MEGALITHIC DWELLINGS

What of actual dwelling places and their construction in the Neolithic period? Certainly many small dwellings would have been made only of some type of thatch over a thin framework of branches, and any remains of these have long since disappeared. But here and there throughout Europe and the British Isles there are isolated examples of carefully constructed megalithic houses. These are exactly as implied, small dwellings constructed from carefully shaped stones of varying sizes, and the few surviving examples are most meticulously built. Probably the best-known site containing this type of building is the megalithic village at Skara Brae. This village of ten dwellings is situated in a most beautiful position close to the shore of the Bay of Skaill on the west coast of Orkney's mainland. Accurate dating has shown that these houses were occupied between 3100 and 2450 BC, and it is primarily due to their location that they are so well preserved. They were designed with stone walls below ground level and prior to excavation the dwellings had filled with sand and domestic rubbish over the ages, thus preserving their interiors almost intact. No doubt they originally had some type of thatched roof, probably of heather around a wooden framework, but no trace of this survives.

Megalithic 'houses' at Skara Brae

Beholding these small stone buildings today, one cannot help but marvel at the ingenuity of the builders; the contents are made entirely from stone – it is like watching the TV programme *The Flintstones*. In one there is a stone hearth edged with slabs, a stone 'dresser' with two shelves, two stone box beds which would have been filled with heather by their occupants, and other basic stone furniture. Taking into consideration the warmer climate of Neolithic times and the fact that these dwellings were sunk into the ground to roof level, they would not have been nearly as uncomfortable as one might think, as well as being adequately protected from the strong Orkney winds. Stone boxes are also in evidence in one of the dwellings and these were originally sealed with clay. Within these troughs were found limpet and cockle shells, suggesting that they were used either for storing or for breeding fish, or perhaps both. Taking into consideration that these dwellings are almost 5000 years old, the ingenuity and skill of their construction are quite extraordinary.

STONE CIRCLE COMPLEXES

A stone circle complex is much more than just a stone circle, having impressive extending stone avenues used for processional purposes, and often large marker stones beyond these. Fine examples of such complexes are Avebury and Stonehenge.

Travelling south-west from the Orkney Isles we find on the Isle of Lewis in the Outer Hebrides or Western Isles the stone circle complex at Callanish. With its enchantingly beautiful setting above the sea loch Loch Roag, it is probably the most beautiful and elaborate Neolithic stone circle complex in existence, having wide stone rows or avenues extending at right angles from the central circle. From the air the outline is of an enormous 'wheel cross', and this was certainly no accidental layout but a carefully designed place for worship and ritual observance. This is an account by Simant Bostock of a visit to Callanish:

In the far north-west reaches of the British Isles, off the coast of Scotland on the edge of the Atlantic Ocean, lie the Hebridean Islands or the Western Isles. Mountain and sea, white sand and rock, peat moorland and heather combine to form one of the most magical and remote areas of Britain. At the northern end of this long chain of islands are the isles of Lewis and Harris, the home of one of the most outstanding and unique prehistoric monuments in Britain – the standing stones of Callanish.

Standing on a ridge of moorland near the west coast of Lewis, overlooking the waters of east Loch Roag, with the moors sweeping away to the distant hills and the mountains of Harris, the tall slender stones of silver Lewissian gneiss rise up beneath the vast expanse of the northern sky. The village of Callanish and its outlying crofts nestle in the moorland beside the stones. These stand like guardians, wise grey elders at the entrance to the Celtic Otherworld. Only the islands of St Kilda and the fairy-inhabited Flannon Islands separate the Western Isles and the stones of Callanish from 1800 kilometres (3000 miles) of ocean.

Callanish stone circle complex

Five thousand years ago this great monument was erected by the Neolithic peoples inhabiting the islands – a spiritual centre in which to perform their religious ceremonies and magical rituals and as a symbol of the power and spirit of their people. A circle of tall standing stones was erected surrounding a giant monolith at its centre, with a small chambered cairn beneath it. An avenue of standing stones was built leading to the circle from the direction just east of north, with three other rows of stones radiating out from the circle, running to the east, the south and the west. The completed monument spreads out like a great Celtic cross, 120 metres (400 ft) long and 46 metres (150 ft) wide. Fingers of stone point into the heavens, marking the journey of the sun, moon and stars through the cycle of the seasons. Images and stories of funeral pyres and sacrifice, the journey of the soul, giants and enchanters and petrified figures, of tribal gatherings and the spirit of the ancestors rise and fade within the mystery surrounding the stones. As with other megalithic sites, their true purpose is obscured in the mists of time.

According to legend, a great king had organized the building of this pagan temple. He had come with a fleet of ships, bringing with him the great stones, together with an entourage of priests and African slaves. The slaves erected the stones, and those who died were buried within the circle. The king then departed, leaving his high priest and others to practise their religious ceremonies and magical rites together with the local inhabitants. The priests were described as wearing robes made of many kinds of feathers. The high priest wore a robe of white feathers with a girdle of luminous mallard neck feathers, and appeared with wrens flying about him.

In the nineteenth century some of the local Hebridean families were described as 'belonging to the stones' and were regarded with high esteem. At Beltane and midsummer people then still visited the stones and it was said that at sunrise something described as 'the Shining One' came to the stones, walking down the avenue heralded by the song of the cuckoo. These visits to the stones continued in secret after a local minister forbade such gatherings, 'for it would not do to neglect the stones,' said the local folk.

The stones of Callanish could well be described as the Shining Ones – their crystalline structure causing them to reflect a silvery light of their own. A deep atmosphere of peace and stillness surrounds the stones, especially at sunrise and in the twilight of the sunset. In the remoteness of the moorland landscape, with the air filled with the drifting scent of the crofters' peat fires, the veil between the worlds is thin. The stones stand guard at the entrance to the spirit world.

STONE CIRCLES

From the middle of the Neolithic era (which ran from *c.* 5000 to *c.* 2200 BC) to the beginning of the Bronze Age (2200 BC–1000 BC) those mysterious structures known as stone circles were being constructed. They have a wide distribution, even though they are most commonly associated with Britain and Ireland. Intersecting stone circles were being built around 2000 BC as far afield as Li Muri in Sardinia, and other examples of single circles can be found in Denmark, Belgium, Czechoslovakia and Portugal.[4] Probably one of the most beautiful sites for a stone circle is Castlerigg in the Lake District; the stones are sited on a high plateau with magnificent views across the mountainous Cumbrian countryside. A number of fine examples in Wales, Cornwall, Ireland and Scotland can still be found, and one such is the magnificently located Ring of Brodgar on the Orkney Isles. Solar, lunar and sometimes even stellar alignments had been evaluated by our ancestors, the most familiar being stone alignments with the sun on the summer solstice or longest day of the year. This is in the same tradition of the chambered cairn builders mentioned earlier, who often aligned the passages of their cairns to the rising sun (or occasionally sunset, as at Maes Howe cairn, also on Orkney) on the winter solstice or shortest day.

An account of the Ring of Brodgar stone circle and the surrounding area is here given by Linda Todd, a resident of the Orkney Isles.

The Orkney Isles, a group of 70 islands situated 32 kilometres (20 miles) off the north coast of Scotland, are rich in prehistory – an archaeologist's paradise. Chambered cairns, standing stones and Neolithic settlements such as Skara Brae, to name but a few, are in evidence on many of the islands. On Orkney mainland the builders of the Ring of Brodgar chose a dramatic and beautiful site on a small strip of land between the lochs of Stenness and Harray to construct this imposing megalithic circle. The mystery of this impressive circle of standing stones is emphasized by the stark moorland on which they stand, silhouetted against the vast backdrop of the northern sky.

Built *c.* 2500 BC, Brodgar, known as the Sun Temple, has the same diameter, 105 metres (340 ft), as the inner ring of Avebury stone circle, 1440 kilometres (900 miles) south in Wiltshire, and has several sun and moon alignments. Only 21 of the original 60 stones remain standing. The deep ditch which surrounds the stone circle is broken by two opposing causeways, one in the north-west and the other in the south-east quadrant of the circle. There are several small mounds in the surrounding area. One of them, Salt Knowe, situated about 90 metres (300 ft) south-west of Brodgar, has been excavated and a burial cist was revealed. Close to the shore of Loch Harray there are two large mounds. Plumcake Barrow, the most northerly of the two, was excavated in the 1850s and two cists were discovered. One of them contained a steatite cinerary urn with cremated bones.

East of Brodgar, on a low platform 12 metres (40 ft) in diameter, stands the monolith known as the Comet Stone. The stumps of two other stones are visible.

Across the Brodgar Bridge, where Stenness and Harray lochs meet and mingle stands the Watch Stone, a huge monolith over six metres (18 ft) high. It is thought that the Watch Stone is associated with the Stones of Stenness. This is a megalithic site visible from the Ring of Brodgar which originally contained 12 upright stones. Only three spectacular stones remain upright today. The original stone circle was 50 metres (160 ft) in diameter and is known as the Moon Temple. In the centre of the circle there is a square setting of stones laid horizontally, and this setting was found to contain fragments of cremated bones, charcoal and shards of grooved-ware pottery. The Stones of Stenness circle was constructed earlier than the Ring of Brodgar and dates from *c.* 3000 BC.

The Ring of Brodgar, Orkney Islands

What do we know of these people who, almost 5000 years ago, raised these stone circles, monuments to the sun and moon? That they lived in village settlements like Skara Brae, and that they buried their dead in cists within mounds like Salt Knowe, and spectacular chambered cairns such as Maes Howe. These last three sites are all in the area close to the stone circles. Did they gather at nature's festival-times to feast and worship?

For those of us who are drawn to these standing stones, to walk from the Sun Temple, the Ring of Brodgar, past the Comet Stone and the Watch Stone to the Moon Temple, the Stones of Stenness, there is an impression of walking a ceremonial path and a feeling of wonder for times past.

DOLMENS

Continuing with our observations of Neolithic monuments in what are now known as the Celtic countries, we take a look at a dolmen in western Ireland. Dolmens, which consist of two or more upright stones with a heavy horizontal capstone, were originally covered with earth, and as such would have been burial chambers. Over a long period of time this covering of soil has been eroded, leaving the inner chamber of large stones open to the heavens. This particular dolmen in County Clare provides a most striking silhouette against the sky, rising as it does from the unearthly landscape of the Burren. Here follows a recent account by Simant Bostock of a visit to the site.

In the west of Ireland, rising from the rugged cliffs of the Atlantic coast-line, lies the Burren region of County Clare. A bleak lunar landscape of gnarled and weathered limestone slabs, without trees or shrubs yet with a unique collection of Arctic, Alpine and Mediterranean flowers that has become internationally famous. Glaciation and erosion over thousands of years has produced this eerie landscape, but there is also evidence that the deforestation employed by the Neolithic and Bronze Age farmers of prehistory contributed to its present day appearance.

The Burren is littered with the remains of these early settlers – dolmens, cairns, wedge-tombs, raths and ring-forts bear testimony to the many different peoples who made their home here. Poulnabrone dolmen is one of the most spectacular of these monuments and probably the most frequently photographed dolmen in the whole of Ireland. Slabs of limestone rise from the stone pavement of the Burren, supporting the large, tilted capstone which forms the small chamber standing at the centre of a low, circular cairn.

Excavations at Poulnabrone in 1986 unearthed the best-preserved burial deposits to be found at any of the numerous Irish dolmens. The finds included the remains of 16–22 adults and six children. The bones found suggested that they had probably been exposed elsewhere before their remains had been taken and placed within the chamber of the shrine. Most of the people were under 30 years old when they died, with the exception of one who was over 40 years old. Other finds consisted of a polished stone axe, two stone beads, a bone pendant and a bone pin, two quartz crystals, flint arrowheads and scrapers and

Poulnabrone dolmen, County Clare

many broken pieces of pottery. The dolmen is said to have been built *c.* 3800 BC and used for about 600 years.

The power of Poulnabrone far exceeds its actual size. The stark simplicity of its structure, rising from the bare rock into the emptiness of the lunar landscape, suggests a piece of modern sculpture. The mysterious and haunting atmosphere of the Burren adds to the sense of the dolmen's being an entrance to another world and another time. Here 5000 years ago the Tuatha Dé Danann, the Shining Ones or fairy folk of Irish legend, performed their magic. Here the people of the Neolithic era placed the remains of their ancestors, visiting the shrine to perform their rituals and ceremonies. Here they made contact with the spirit world, perhaps placating the gods with sacrifice to ensure the fertility of their crops, their livestock and their clan; also honouring the power of the sun, moon and stars, which had given them life. Here, perhaps, the shaman or medicine man of the tribe would talk with the spirits of the ancestors or the gods through trance or divination, providing guidance and reassurance for the uncertainties of their short and precarious lives.

Today the Burren stands grey and empty, swept by the winds and rain from the Atlantic Ocean. The figures and voices fade into the crevices of the rock and sink into the mist, leaving us to speculate on the lives of our brothers and sisters of 5000 years ago, their world outlook and their spiritual beliefs. Here at Poulnabrone we are haunted by the closeness of their presence yet frustrated by the abyss of time and silence that stands between us.

STANDING STONES

One further megalithic monument frequently found in today's Celtic countries and across Europe is the standing stone. These vary enormously in size, and are even more widely distributed than stone circles. They range in size from the massive menhir at Dol, on the borders of Normandy and Brittany, which is just over nine metres (30 ft) high, to numerous smaller ones located throughout Britain, France, Spain and Scandinavia. Their erection continued through the Neolithic era and into the Early Bronze Age, which began *c.* 2200 BC.

The purpose of many of these stones is still uncertain. However, some are obvious alignments with natural features in the landscape, used in combination with sunrise or sunset at one of the four major seasonal festivals, or at the four Celtic fire-festivals of Beltane, Lugnasadh, Samhain and Imbolc. Some may have been used purely as guides for land or sea travellers, being visible from a great distance. Other theories put forward include that they were the focal point for clan gatherings; that their shadows were measured in order to plot the path of the seasons (which seems more than likely); that they were markers for the burial sites of long-dead rulers or chieftains; and that some of the large standing stones, such as the Grand Menhir at Er Grah, in Brittany, were used as lunar observatories in conjunction with other standing stones visible from it. This latter might sound a little far-fetched, but the calculations worked out around Er Grah are astonishingly accurate.[5]

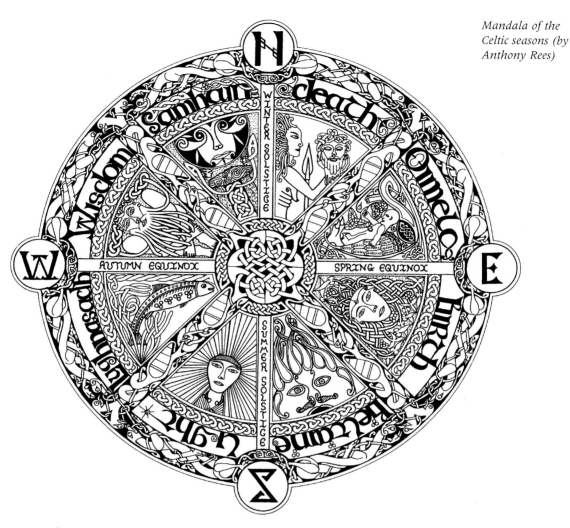

Mandala of the Celtic seasons (by Anthony Rees)

Standing stones abound in western Scotland, and three particular ones on the island of North Uist are described here by Alan Pratt, a resident of this Hebridean island:

North Uist is part of a group of islands situated off the western coast of Scotland which are collectively known as the Outer Hebrides. Despite the island's small size – about 16 by 24 kilometres (ten by 15 miles), nearly half of which is either fresh water or sea lochs – it plays host to well over 60 ancient sites, ranging from stone circles, chambered cairns, standing stones and crosses to aisled houses, souterrains, duns, brochs, chapels, temples, villages and even a potter's workshop, which is considered to be the oldest in Europe.

With regard to standing stones, the 1928 Royal Commission on Ancient and Historical Monuments and Constructions of Scotland identified no less than 19 on North Uist. The current Ordnance Survey map of the area marks ten of these, most of which are to be found close to the sea, nearly all of them with either a cairn or a burial chamber close by. This has led to the belief that many of the standing stones are actually monuments to long-dead kings or warriors. All of the stones have a tale to tell. I have chosen three sites which I feel are a representative sample of both the types of stone and the folklore surrounding them.

One of the largest and most impressive stones is that known as Clach Mor an Che, the Big Stone of the World, which stands at the edge of the seashore (not far from one of the only two pubs on North Uist, the Westford Inn). It stands just over two and a half metres (eight ft) high and 76 centimetres (30 in) wide. On the first occasion that I visited the stone, the sun was just setting and small waves were lapping on the seashore – an idyllic scene if ever there was one. And yet folklore has it that local recalcitrants were tied to the stone for their wrongdoings. Some punishment! Although if it were during the summertime, the local midges, renowned for their ferocity, would no doubt have inflicted their own brand of punishment upon the wrong-doers! Not far from the stone are the remains of a chambered cairn called Dun na Cairnaich, and at least one historian has suggested that the cairn and the standing stone were monuments to Che, one of the seven sons of Crithne, an ancestor of the Picts, who is said to have been buried there following his death in battle.

About six kilometres (four miles) away, high on a hillside overlooking Clach Mor an Che, stands another stone about the same height as the previous one but much wider, and set at an angle facing south. The stone is visible from the road, and I had driven past it on many occasions but had never stopped to walk up the hillside to visit it. On the first occasion that I did, I could see a couple of irregular shapes on top of the stone. As I drew closer, these two shapes suddenly flapped their wings and two ravens flew in opposite directions from the stone. I mention this because while researching the history of this stone in the local library, I found that the name of the stone was Clach Bharnach

Standing stones on North Uist: Clach Mor an Che (left) and Clach Bharnach (right)

Bhraodag, which means the Limpet Stone of Freya. The name Freya betrays the strong Norse influence on these islands, and according to Norse mythology it was Freya who taught Odin a shamanistic magic called Seidhr, and it was Odin who was able to communicate with the two ravens who gave him the ability to 'have knowledge of all things, in all places'. There is a Gaelic saying, '*Tha tios fithich agad*', which means, 'You have more knowledge and understanding than is natural.' The literal translation, however, is, 'You have the raven's knowledge.'

Not far from Lochmaddy, on the western side of Bashaval, stand three stones called Na Fir Bhreige, or the False Men, which are set in a straight line. Although not as impressive in size as the stones previously described, they are worth noting for the tale that is told about them. Apparently three Isle of Skye men abandoned their wives and travelled over to Uist, planning to start a new life. Their actions came to the attention of the local witch, who (presumably as an act of female solidarity) placed a spell on them, and as the men made their way across the hillside, they were turned into stone. They stand there to this day as a reminder (and presumably a warning) to any man who may be contemplating a similar course of action!

Folklore and mythology aside, however, the early work of Professor Thom[6] gives a modern insight into the origins and uses of the standing stones. While Thom does not dispute the fact that the stones were used for burial rituals and ceremonial gatherings, his surveys and astronomical data suggest that the stones were used in conjunction with cairns and naturally occurring marker points to fix ritual and ceremonial dates. His surveys in North Uist have shown that the stones and their alignments can be used to set the dates of the vernal equinox, sunset, midwinter sunrise, Beltane, Samhain and various other pre-Celtic and Celtic festivals.

It is quite probable that we shall never fully unravel the mysteries that surround the stones and their uses, but the fact that we are still drawn to and affected by them suggests that we retain a little of the faith of the original builders deep within our memories – a faith which will not only ensure continued reverence for these ancient sites but also a continued reverence for life itself.

ANCIENT SITES AND THE
ANIMAL KINGDOM

Folklore and legend often associate ancient sites with animals or birds as their 'guardians'. Whatever one's views on this matter, it does seem that even today many sites possess an atmosphere which is peaceful, healing and also attracts various forms of wildlife. Often there seems to be no apparent reason for an animal or bird to be in this vicinity, but it will return so frequently or remain so close by that one cannot call it coincidence. In the picture here, the wild horses are grazing around the ancient stones of Shovel Down Stone Row, near Scorhill on Dartmoor. Although there is a vast expanse of open grazing for them on the moors, they prefer to remain most of the time in the vicinity of the stones.

*Wild horses at
Shovel Down
stone row,
Dartmoor*

The following account of similar phenomena is by someone who at first felt very sceptical about the whole idea, but subsequently became considerably more open-minded:

Many years ago when my interest in the Celts was beginning to stir, I read in a couple of unusual and interesting books about the relationship between ancient sacred places and certain animals. From Neolithic stone circles and standing stones to early Celtic chapels and carved crosses, all these were said to exude an atmosphere which attracted certain kinds of animals. The reasons given were, to me at the time, rather 'pie in the sky'. One book said that in Celtic folklore 'the souls of departed worshippers at these sites are said to return in animal form to watch over and protect them'.

I remember thinking at the time that this sounded rather naïvely amusing, and that perhaps on the next page I would read that pigs actually could fly! It wasn't until I went to live in Scotland on the Kintyre peninsula that my perceptions changed a little on the subject.

Shortly after I moved there I made a visit to a very remote sixth-century chapel at Skipness. The tiny ruined building is called Kilbrannan Chapel. The name Kilbrannan means the cell or church of St Brendan, the Irish saint and navigator. The location of this chapel is extremely remote and equally beautiful, being on the seashore and overlooking the northerly tip of the Isle of Arran, whose mist-shrouded mountains rise almost sheer out of the sea to over 600 metres (2000 ft). It was February when I visited, and as usual I had with me sketch pad and pencil. Even though it was mid-afternoon, the temperature was barely above zero, and with a strong breeze I recall my hand being completely numb after ten minutes' work.

This is a digression though. As I approached, there was one solitary seal positioned on a rock. He wasn't just 'there', he was watching me very carefully. Anyone who has observed a seal at reasonably close quarters and seen those large, liquid black eyes will know what I mean. He was still there when I left, and still watching me. Later that night I thought of the books I'd read, but still told myself that this was a 'one-off' coincidence.

Not so long afterwards I visited Southend, on the southernmost tip of the Mull of Kintyre. Here there is another very early ruined Celtic chapel, which is also home to 'St Columba's footprints', a rock with two footprints carved into it on the site where St Columba is said to have first landed on his exile from Ireland in AD 563. Here again at Southend close to the chapel were two solitary seals on a rock, just watching me. It certainly makes you respect a sacred site even more if you feel that your every movement is being carefully monitored by seals, and a brief thought that they might be embodied Celtic monks certainly went through my mind!

Suffice to say that most early chapels and also several Celtic crosses on Kintyre are very close to the seashore, and on nine visits out of ten I encountered the watchful seal or two. St Columba's cave near Tarbert was another identical experience, with one lone seal watching me from a little island at the edge of the loch.

This was a number of years ago, and I hadn't thought of the subject again until a friend who lives on North Uist told me of two ravens who, whenever he visited a particular standing stone on the island, were perched on it, even though there were no trees for a good distance and their nightly roosting place was far from there.

Recently I made a visit to one of the stone circles in the area of Dorset in which I live. This particular one near Portesham is in a magnificent location, high on a remote hill overlooking the sea, with Chesil Beach almost below, St Catherine's Chapel near Abbotsbury in the distance to the west, looking very like Glastonbury Tor on its terraced hill, and Portland Bill about ten kilometres (six miles) due east, reaching into a vivid blue sea. As I was standing on the stile of the enclosure to the circle, admiring this wonderful place, a fox calmly walked out of the hedge to the side of me, not more than five metres (15 ft) away. I remained perfectly still, expecting it to run rapidly away. Instead, the animal actually walked towards me and turned to look directly at me when not more than three metres (ten ft) away. This gave me the most uncanny feeling of being 'checked out' by the fearless animal. I think it must have decided that my intentions were good, as it then slowly trotted off down the remote track at a very leisurely pace.

So, are animals attracted by the atmospheres of ancient sacred places? Do souls of past worshippers, now in animal form, keep a watchful eye on these sites, as Celtic folklore relates? Who knows? I now remain very open-minded.

A HUMAN PORTRAIT

Neolithic/Bronze Age man (contemporary sculpture by Simant Bostock)

To conclude this section on Neolithic and Early Bronze Age sites in today's Celtic countries, I had wanted to include an illustration representative of Neolithic man himself in near-authentic surroundings. None of the pictures I found seemed to fully convey the real essence of early man, and it was not until I visited an exhibition of sculpture in Glastonbury recently that I came across this image here, which struck me very forcibly. Having inquired of its creator what inspired him to produce the fine (and very large) relief work in plaster and collage, I was told that it had been christened Bog Man, and was influenced mainly by the following: Tollund Man, a fairly recently excavated and fully preserved body from the peat bogs of Denmark, dating from *c.* 200 BC, and the Upton Lovel shaman, the body of a man found buried in a Wiltshire round barrow with grave goods including a necklace of bone points and some crystal balls, dating from *c.* 1500 BC. The designs on the cave walls of this sculpture were inspired by a visit to the interior of the Newgrange chambered cairn in County Meath, and the shells and bones strewn over the cave floor were said to be representative of the diet of Neolithic man.

For me it is the most accurate representation I have yet seen.

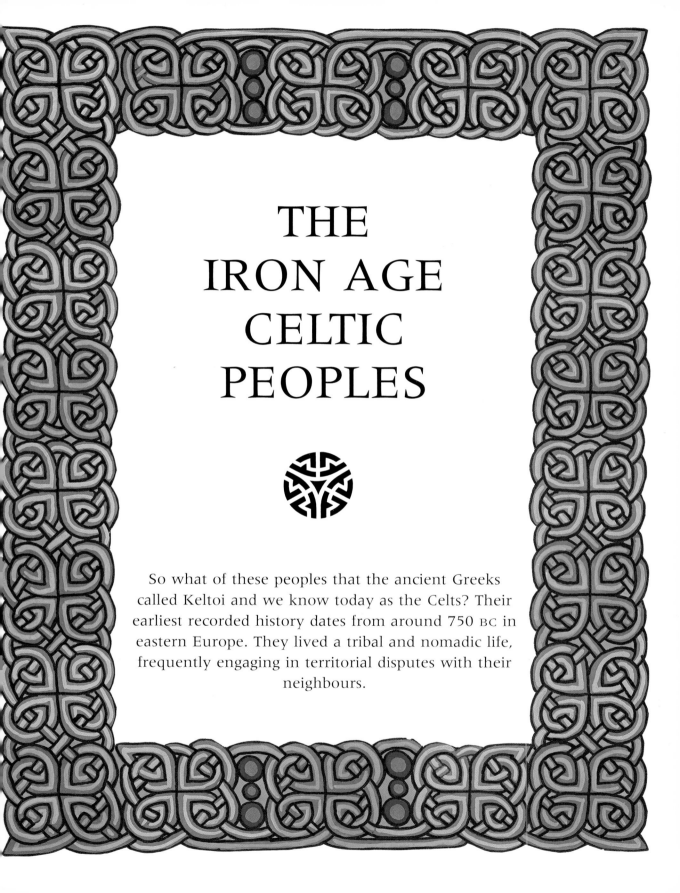

THE IRON AGE CELTIC PEOPLES

So what of these peoples that the ancient Greeks called Keltoi and we know today as the Celts? Their earliest recorded history dates from around 750 BC in eastern Europe. They lived a tribal and nomadic life, frequently engaging in territorial disputes with their neighbours.

THE CELTS IN AUSTRIA

D uring the seventh and sixth centuries BC, Hallstatt, a large prehistoric salt-mining area in Austria, was one of their main territories. The following account of the Celts in this region is by Dr Jutta Nordone a historian/folklorist who lives in the area.

Austria is one of the oldest Celtic territories in Europe. The Hallstatt period, 750–480/450 BC, was named after a salt-mining village in Upper Austria which was an important settlement in that time. The best-known Austrian site from the later Celtic La Tène period, c. 500–300 BC, is at Dürrnberg, near Salzburg. Within both these regions the wealth of the Celtic people was based on salt-mining, and in the latter the mountains held five different areas of mining dating from about the same period. A huge area five kilometres (three miles) in length and with a maximum depth of 250 metres (812 ft) was mined by the Celts at this time. Salt-mining did not stop after the Celts, but has played an important part in Austria for centuries, as it still does today. The word 'Hall', often to be found in place-names or geographical features in Austria, is Celtic for salt. The Dürrnberg site was discovered in the nineteenth century but no major excavations took place until 1910. In 1932 a disturbed burial of a Celtic chieftain was discovered by Oliver Close and this contained the famous Dürrnberg beaked pitcher, a masterpiece of early Celtic craftsmanship dating from 400 BC. A detail of the carving from the handle is illustrated here. The following years brought systematic excavations. For instance, the campaign of 1978–82, necessitated by plans to build a road through the Celtic settlement, brought to light the living quarters of the artisans of the village. The Dürrnberg pitcher and many other beautiful and interesting Celtic objects can be seen in the nearby Keltenmuseum in Hallein, which is also the Dürrnberg Research Centre, founded in 1984. It is complemented by an open-air museum with reconstructed Celtic dwellings, outhouses and stables, etc., and is a valuable addition. The museum is situated on Dürrnberg mountain itself and can be reached by cable car from Hallein.

Celtic settlements in eastern Austria are much less known than the well-documented ones in the west or centre of the country. A most interesting exhibition in 1992, 'The Celts in Eastern Austria', proved that, contrary to traditional archaeological opinion, tribes in eastern Austria, west Hungary and the southern parts of the Czech and Slovak republics were not 'Celticized' by way of conquest (as, for instance, in the Celtic migrations of 390 BC onwards) but were part of a region of early Celtic development ranging from eastern France to the Carpathian Mountains as early as 450 BC. This eastern variation and its characteristics in culture, art and religion were very well documented in the exhibition through already well-known objects such as the bronze situla of Kuffern, a decorated bronze pail for carrying liquids from Lower Austria with fine Celtic ornamentation, but also through the latest finds from excavated sites in the central and eastern regions of Lower Austria like Frazhausen, Ossarn and sites near the Hungarian border. Trade in these settlements was based on the exchange of goods, similar to other centres in Austria, but they did not have salt as at Dürrnberg, or iron ore like the Celtic kingdom of

Detail from the Dürrnberg pitcher

Noricum in central Austria (which became a Roman province of the same name in the year 9 BC).

This eastern region is, however, rich agricultural country and especially favourable for grape-growing and wine-making, which is still the main industry there today. Discovery of prehistoric grape-pips and artefacts seems to indicate an ancient tradition. The existence and growth of early villages could be due to the production of wine.

Hallstatt, Dürrnberg and the newly discovered sites in Lower Austria are still the object of archaeological research today. Every year brings new excavations and discoveries and a better knowledge of Austria's Celtic past.

THE LA TÈNE ERA

Progressively in the fifth century BC the La Tène area became a focus for the Celts. La Tène is a Swiss lakeside settlement on Lake Neuchâtel. The finely developed metalwork from this era is well known, and the style continued throughout Europe until at least the first century BC. Artefacts such as bronze mirrors with La Tène ornamentation have also been found in various British excavations. The Celts of this era were flamboyant warfaring tribes, with a love of brightly coloured clothing and ornamentation. Examples of enamelled horse brasses, chariot decorations and brooches of fine craftsmanship can be found in museums in Britain and Europe. It should be remembered that the

Fifth-century-BC La Tène gold jewellery: 'face' brooch from Slovenske Pravno and 'satyr' figure from Erstfeld, Switzerland (contemporary reproductions by Simant Bostock)

43

Celts were experts with regard to horses and horsemanship, and the chariot itself was an early Celtic invention which provided them with much success in battle. In the Celtic belief system, the horse was worshipped as Epona, the horse goddess. Various small effigies of horses in pottery and metal have been found at Celtic sites in Europe, and the large hillside carvings in chalk soil, such as the White Horse of Uffington, near Oxford, also testify to this cult.

The Celts believed in 'shape-shifting': this meant that the gods were able to appear in animal form as they chose. Other animals were also considered sacred and regarded as 'totems'. The wild boar was a symbol of ferocity both physically and visually, and the Celts believed that its spirit would make their warriors fierce in battle. As well as helmets with boar sculptures on them, some fine free-standing sculptures of the boar have been found, including a magnificent bronze from Neuvy-en-Sullias in France, which dates from the first century BC. Likewise the bull, the salmon, the eagle and the stag all had their own attributes and powers.

Celtic wild boar (contemporary sculpture by Simant Bostock based on first-century-BC Celtic boar)

Cernunnos, Lord of the Animals (contemporary sculpture by Simant Bostock based on figure from Gundestrup Cauldron, first century BC)

Lord over all the animals was Cernunnos, the horned god, who was seen by the Celts as the ruler of the natural kingdom. The fine work of Celtic craftsmanship called the Gundestrup Cauldron, a large silver vessel found in Denmark and dating from the first century BC, carries an image of him with antlers on his head, sitting cross-legged with a torque in his right hand and a snake or serpent in his left. The torque, being circular, is said to symbolize infinity, or the never-ending cycle of death and rebirth.

Sarah King, a resident of Luxemburg, writes about the Celts who lived in the Ardennes region, and also their presence in Burgundy, France, during the La Tène period:

The early Celts occupied the area of the Ardennes in western Europe, and in 1993 an exhibition of 100 Celtic artefacts was held at the Trier Rheinisches Landesmuseum. From 600 BC the Celts settled in the Ardennes region, trading with the Mediterranean people, most notably the Etruscans. The Ardennes, which border on the River Moselle to the west, are reputed to be lean in Celtic history. However, on the summer solstice today one can witness the lighting of the St John's Day fire on Mont du Moulin, near Séry, north-east of Rethel. Not only is this Celtic tradition observed every year, but there is also a local legend that the mountains of Séry were created by the giant Gargantus (Gargan, the Celtic god of earth) when he shook off some soil that clung to his foot. A Celtic road ran through the Porcien valley from Reims (Roman Durocortorum) to the town of Charleville-Mézières and on into the Ardennes.

Burgundy is an area of France also steeped in Celtic history. By the sixth century BC Hallstatt Celts had established themselves on Mont Lassois, just north of Châtillon-sur-Seine. They were wealthy enough not only to acquire treasures but to bury them with their dead. The three-metre-square (10-ft) grave of the lady who became known as the Princess of Vix contained a bronze Grecian wine vase or krater 1.64 metres (five ft four in) high and weighing 208.6 kilos (33 stones).

Reconstruction of murus Gallicus at Vertault

Nothing of this age or size has survived in Greece. A bas-relief portraying soldiers and horse-drawn chariots encircles the top of the vase. Several horse's heads turn from the procession to look at you. Each of the two handles features a Gorgon. A female figure forms the handle of the sieve-like lid. There is some speculation as to why the Celts would have acquired a vessel for mixing wine (perhaps with herbs), since they didn't produce wine themselves in this area.

The body of the princess was laid on a four-wheeled wagon and adorned with a unique 24-carat gold torc weighing 480 grams (just over one lb), amber jewellery and Celtic La Tène-style brooches. Two Attic bowls were among the rich store of artefacts buried with her. The Vix treasure is significant for two reasons: it gives evidence of the trade between the Celts and the Greek and Etruscan worlds, and it attests to the importance a Celtic woman could have. This last aspect was later illustrated by, among others, the mighty Queen Boudicca of the Iceni Celtic tribe in southern Britain in the first century AD.

The Vix site on the River Seine was excavated in 1953. It was returned to agricultural use after the treasure had been removed to the Musée Archéologique at Châtillon-sur-Seine. Also at this small but excellent museum are artefacts unearthed at Vertault (Vertillium), 20 kilometres (12 miles) west of Mont Lassois. An attempt has been made to make this site accessible to visitors. To this end a Celtic wall (*murus Gallicus*) was constructed according to Julius Caesar's description in his *Gallic Wars*. Caesar was impressed by the ability of the Celtic wall to withstand both ramming and fire. He even added that it was attractive.

THE ARRIVAL OF THE CELTS IN BRITAIN

Venturing further afield in the fourth century BC, the Celts settled in northern Italy and invaded Rome in their warlike fashion around 390 BC. Their itinerant and warfaring natures took them as far as Greece, where an invasion of Delphi is recorded in 297 BC. Soon after this a group of Celts travelled even further, into Galatia, and subsequently settled there (see page 14).

During the second century BC, Roman military forces increased in strength. First southern and central France and subsequently the north was conquered, with Julius Caesar's army finishing off resistance in Gallia Belgica in the middle of the first century BC. The Celts were forced to travel even further north.

It was during this time that many Celts arrived in Britain. From the second century BC onwards, they are known to have established tribal communities throughout the land and about 33 of these are historically recorded.

Yet it is also possible that as early as 2000 BC tribes with Celtic origins already existed in both Britain and Ireland, and were slowly joined and enlarged by traders and nomadic warriors from Europe. The main tin-trading route from Asia Minor to Cornwall, the Phoenician Trading Route, had been in existence since pre-Roman times, and almost certainly some Celtic migrants came to Britain by this way. At that time Cornwall was the largest tin-producing country in the western world.

CELTIC COINAGE

As the Celtic tribes were nomadic, their main possessions needed to be easily transportable. According to the Greek historian Polybius, writing *c*. 140 BC, the Celts' main possessions were livestock and gold. It seems probable that their adoption of coinage was due to their contact with the Greek and Roman civilizations, whose coinage systems were already well established. Here we have historian Frank James's view on this subject:

> Between around 500 BC and the first century AD, the Celts were one of the most widespread and influential peoples in Europe. They stretched from Britain as far afield as Galatia (which means 'land of the Celts'). They were well known to classical writers both Greek and Roman, who give us much fascinating information about their character and customs. We read that:

> They live in unwalled villages, without any superfluous
> furniture; for as they slept on beds of leaves, and fed on meat, and
> were extensively occupied with war and agriculture, their lives
> were very simple. . . . Their possessions consisted of cattle and gold,
> because these were the only things they could carry about
> with them everywhere according to the circumstances, and shift
> where they chose.
> (Polybius, *Histories*, 2.17, 8–12)

Cattle and gold . . . Though their great gold torcs are familiar to most of us and continue to be rescued from under the plough by fortunate farmers, Celtic coinage is perhaps less familiar. The Celts' own interest in 'money' probably stemmed from their widespread use as mercenaries across the ancient world. Renowned as they were for valour in battle, kings or city-states were prepared to employ them in time of war to fight on their side, and to reward them with money in the same way that they rewarded their own troops, with, however, slight differences.

In the ancient Greek world every city had its own coinage, valid in its own ports and markets but needing usually to be changed into the currency of another city before it could be used there, rather as we change money at country borders. Before the days of Rome, whose coinage was circulated throughout the Empire, the one notable exception to this rule was the coinage of Alexander the Great, whose conquests took him right across the Greek world and well into India. His own coins as a result became the most widely recognized and accepted of any, even after his death in 323 BC, and it must have been for this reason that the first coins of the Celts were copies of Alexander's coinage. There was a significant difference, however; virtually all coins in the Greek world were of silver, whereas the Celts preferred theirs to be minted in gold. It was not until later that the use of silver and bronze became common, as a result of contact with the Romans.

Celtic coinage continues to be the subject of much research and debate. Our knowledge of its use and distribution, in the absence of written sources, depends entirely upon archaeology. Coins 'travel'

Gold stater from the Atrebates tribe, first century BC

very easily, and were of course undated in our sense of the term. Also in most cases they carry little or no inscription, so it is easy to see how the subject can be something of a minefield! Yet they are fascinating because of the light they shed on an important and unique period in the history not only of our country but of Europe as a whole. Indeed, in the absence of written records they are one of our most important sources for this period.

The gold 'stater' was one of the most highly prized of Celtic coins. There are many designs of these, each relating to individual regions of both Britain and Europe. The coin illustrated is a British gold 'stater' from the Atrebates tribe, and dates from the first century BC.

At a later date silver coinage of a lower denomination was used for day-to-day transactions. The high value of a gold stater may be gauged by the fact that on one occasion we read of soldiers being paid one gold stater each for an entire campaign.

A third and even lower denomination Celtic coin was available in the form of 'potin' money. These coins were minted in strips, which were then cut into weighed units. Potin coins were made from a tin alloy, much of the tin coming from the Cornish tin mines.

CELTIC HILLFORTS

The era in which the Celts arrived in Britain is known as the Iron Age. This period runs from *c.* 1000 BC to AD 43, when it comes to an abrupt halt with the Roman invasion of the country. Some of the Celts' main places of occupation were the Iron Age hillforts. A number of these sites had been in existence in some form or other since Neolithic times, the main reason being that they were in strategic positions with far-reaching views, thus any threat of invasion could be seen well in advance. Also due to their location, they could be relatively easily surrounded with a high wooden fence, which as well as containing the inhabitants would have enclosed their livestock. Stock-rearers from the Bronze Age are also known to have inhabited a number of these magnificent sites.

However, it was only with the advent of the Celts that these forts were reinforced and made secure (or so they thought) with the massive earthen ramparts that are still prominent features of the landscape today. The finest hillforts are in southern and western Britain, and the largest of all, Maiden Castle, is in Dorset, just over a kilometre (about one mile) from Dorchester. (In Roman times, Dorchester was a sizeable town known as Durnovaria; traces of the name are still found there today in, for example, Durngate Street.)

Maiden Castle is the largest Iron Age Celtic hillfort in Europe, with a huge enclosed area of over 16 hectares (40 acres). The entrance 'gate' is a maze-like construction consisting of a series of protective earthen ramparts designed to confuse any invaders and provide the Celts with opportunity for adequate defence. As can be seen from the illustration on page 50, the interior was highly suitable for keeping livestock, as well as protecting a thriving Celtic community. There are several dew-ponds which provided good sources of water, and the faint ridge across the enclosure, visible towards the far end, is the remains of a much earlier and more basic Neolithic construction built about 2000 years earlier on this same site. In Iron Age Britain these forts are said to have been occupied by Celts from as early as 400 BC, though the main occupation and rebuilding took place from the second century BC onwards. They were religious centres as well as being defensive enclosures, and within many of them craft work and production of goods took place. They were focal points for the tribe of the area, and the chief of the tribe would have held sway within the compound. By the first century BC the whole of Britain was divided into Celtic tribal regions, approximately 33 in total. The area based around Maiden Castle was occupied by the Durotriges, while their next-door neighbours, the Atrebates (see page 49) used Silchester (Callera Atrebatum) as their focus. From the Brigantes in northern England to the

Maiden Castle Iron Age hillfort, from the air

Dumnonii in the south-west, these tribes occupied and defended their particular regions, sometimes fighting their neighbours to defend boundaries. By the beginning of the first century AD structured Celtic communities had built up, each with their own craftworkers, coinage and tribal ruler.

Further west than Maiden Castle, yet still in the territory of the Durotriges, is the spectacular Celtic hillfort of Eggardon (*don* or *dun* is Celtic for hill, the same word being found in Gaelic place-names of western Scotland, such as Dunadd in Argyll). Eggardon hillfort is at the very end of a long chalk ridge which runs right across the south of England. Visibility is astonishing on a clear day: the sea is in sight to the south and to the west, as the land drops away, the occupants could look out as far as the borders of their neighbouring tribe, the Dumnonii, who occupied what is now Devon and Cornwall. In the illustration below, the line of the Roman road which ran from Isca

Eggardon Iron Age hillfort, from the air

(Exeter) to Durnovaria (Dorchester) can clearly be seen. It is still a single track, although today it is covered over with tarmac.

Most of these spectacular hillforts are still well preserved today. Unfortunately, though, their Celtic occupants were rapidly and completely routed by the Roman invasion of Britain, which commenced in AD 43. Their elaborate maze-style gateways, such as the one at Maiden Castle, may well have protected the Celts from minor attacks but were no match for an organized military force like the Roman army, which in a very short time defeated entire Celtic communities, taking over and occupying their lands.

The religious use of these hillforts was perpetuated by the superstitious Romans, and on a number of them, including Maiden Castle, there are the remains of Romano-British temples. Their dedication is uncertain; it may well have been a continuation of the Celtic Goddess theme, possibly through fear of incurring the wrath of the deities of the peoples they had ousted. Excavations at the Maiden Castle temple have revealed fragments of a statue of Diana, as well as a bronze three-horned bull with three Goddess figures on its back,[7] indicating links with the Celtic Triple Goddess cult (see page 14).

Iron Age round houses: Castell Henllys (top) and Craggaunowen (bottom)

CELTIC DWELLINGS

What of the actual dwelling places of the Celts in Britain in the Iron Age? In lowland Britain the most frequently occurring style is the familiar 'round house'. These were constructed around a central pole, with a radiating timber frame secured to vertical posts sunk into the ground. The structure was then thatched and the low walls constructed from wattle and daub. Groups of these round houses formed villages in many areas of the lowlands, where wood for their construction was plentiful. Thatched animal shelters and storerooms have also been excavated within these Celtic village communities. Today some fine reconstructions can be visited, including Castell Henllys, near Newport in Dyfed; Craggaunowen, near Quin in County Clare, Ireland, which as well as having Iron Age round houses has a reconstructed crannog or lake dwelling, and a ring fort; and New Barn Field Centre, a 'working' Iron Age homestead not far from Maiden Castle in Dorset.

Another fascinating place where these thatched dwellings can be explored is the Welsh Folk Museum at St Fagans, near Cardiff. The round houses in the Celtic village here are reconstructions of the excavated remains of Iron Age buildings from Clwyd and Gwynedd. Weaving looms, fire-dogs and everyday utensils can be seen inside the houses. Here is a brief description of a visit by Paul Thomas to the village in winter:

At St Fagans in south Wales, just west of Cardiff, is situated the Welsh Folk Museum. Old farmhouses, cottages, shops and other buildings from all over Wales have been brought here and re-erected to give a good idea of life in the old, and not-so-old days. Among the exhibits is the reconstruction of a Celtic village.

I visited St Fagans at the end of November after a light snowfall. It was freezing and there were few visitors, but the weather gave an indication of what it might have been like in winter in the time of the Celts.

The village consists of three round huts surrounded by a wattle fence. This was erected to keep cattle away from the huts, according to the information board outside. It would not have been any use as a defensive construction. The walls of the huts and the doors are low; each hut has a high, conical, thatched roof. Inside, the fireplace was in the centre, and inhabitants slept on platforms slightly raised off the earth floor. There were numerous gaps in the walls and roof.

One of the huts seems to have been used as a barn for the cattle, and there was also a hay barn and chicken coop, although the hens were roaming freely. A guide was lighting a fire in one of the huts, which had two shields with Celtic designs on either side of the doorway. The white woodsmoke completely filled the interior of the roof, giving the impression of a false ceiling! If there was a ventilation hole at the apex then it wasn't very adequate, and the gaps in the building served as another smoke outlet. The fire at this time of year gave little warmth, but being centrally situated everyone would have had a fair share. You could picture the inhabitants huddled around the blazing logs on a winter's night, wrapped in furs and exchanging stories or songs in the flickering light . . . if they weren't too cold to do so!

Presumably with an adequate supply of thatching material the gaps in the original Celtic houses would not have existed and, as anyone who has tried constructing a similar dwelling will testify, if enough ventilation can be provided in the roof, a small fire can generate a considerable amount of heat, if all major sources of draughts are eliminated by filling them with organic material such as straw or bracken. Some of the larger round houses of the Celtic era which have been excavated even had porches with a double door, one serving as a 'fire door' when closed, preventing the wind from blowing sparks on to the interior of the thatch.

These round houses were abundant in the low-lying areas where wood was plentiful. However, in the more remote and austere regions stone was used as the main building material, and often the dwellings were partially sunk into the ground for further protection against the elements. One such stone village exists at Chysauster in Cornwall and was occupied from the first century BC until AD 300. Another Cornish stone village is Carn Euny, whose buildings date from the same period. Both these remote and wild locations would have avoided the impact of the Roman invasion. Another frequently occurring Cornish Iron Age building is the fogou or 'earthhouse'. These underground stone constructions were often linked to a hut above the ground, and may have been used mainly for storage purposes.

Two other fascinating sites containing stone-built Iron Age dwellings are the villages at Jarlshof and Clickhimin, both on the Shetland Isles. Together, these two sites cover a remarkable span of continuous occupation from the Late Neolithic right through to the Middle Ages. During the site's continuous evolution, a Bronze Age smithy was in operation at Jarlshof.

TREES AND THEIR RELEVANCE

The belief system of the Celts was based around the natural world and all its manifestations, so understandably great significance was attached to trees. Imagine life over 2000 years ago. The only living thing on the earth which you knew survived considerably longer than yourself was the tree, so on a very basic level there would have been mystique and a sacredness attached to trees.

The Goidelic alphabet, originating in Ireland and used by the druids, the elders of the Celtic tribes, was known as ogham script. Some Celtic historians refer to this as the Beth-Luis-Nion alphabet.[8] Representations of ogham at a later date can be found on standing stones (see page 68). This alphabet was incorporated within 13 'timespans' which formed the basis of a yearly calendar, and each of these timespans was directly linked to its seasonal tree. The carved inscriptions of ogham on stones is said to have begun in the third century AD, but the script itself is much older. It is mentioned in some of the early Irish sagas, but as the druidic tradition and teachings were strictly oral, we have no direct written evidence of its existence at an earlier date.

To discuss the attributes and properties, as well as the customs and beliefs, surrounding all the 13 trees is beyond the scope of this book, but two particular trees, still regarded with reverence by many, are discussed here.

The first is the yew, which was appropriately associated with the winter solstice (Yule) by the Celtic elders. The second is the oak, still linked today in many people's minds with the druids and their sacred groves. The oak was linked in the Celtic seasonal calendar to the summer solstice.[9]

A general account of the yew tree follows, based around the pioneering work of Allen Meredith, who has single-handedly over a number of years been able to prove conclusively that the yew tree is far older than was originally accepted, and is probably one of the oldest species of tree in the whole world.[10]

Yew trees have always had a mythical power. In pagan times they were worshipped as one of the most sacred trees. The winter solstice in the druids' calendar was represented by a yew. The tree retained a prominent position in Christian culture and is now found in church-yards all over Britain. But to Allen Meredith, housemaster at a Hertfordshire school, the power of the yew tree is far from mythical. A number of years ago he had a series of extraordinary dreams. In them he saw hooded men sitting in a circle, and through a mist he saw a tree which he recognized as a yew. He woke up reciting strange words and remembered that he had been asked to find 'the tree of the cross'.

'At the time I had no idea what the dream meant,' says Meredith. His desire to find out set him on a lifelong investigation into the origins of the yew tree. And his discoveries have forced dendrochronologists (scientists who study the age of trees) to reassess their calculations on the age of yews. This in turn has opened a debate on the influence of paganism on Christianity and cast doubt on the traditional explanation for the location of many of Britain's churches.

Meredith's quest started in the 1970s, when he began to compile a list of old yew trees in the British Isles, travelling to thousands of churches in the process. Many of the locations were listed in a 1946 book entitled *The Churchyard Yew and Immortality*. Through his travels he came to the conclusion that many of the yews in Britain were far older than was realized. Some, he believed, were more than 1000 years old.

At the time the received academic wisdom was that trees in Britain could live for only hundreds of years, not thousands. The 1983 *Encyclopaedia Britannica* says that the idea that the yew could live beyond 1000 years was 'based on the fusion of close-growing trunks [of a number of trees], none of which is more than 250 years old'. W. J. Bean's botanical work *Trees and Shrubs Hardy in the British Isles* claims that the maximum lifespan of yew trees is 800 years. 'When I mentioned to people that trees like this were really a 1000 years old or more, no one really wanted to know,' says Meredith.

One piece of circumstantial evidence that gave his theories real credibility was as follows. He noticed that the Saxon builders of a church in Tandridge, Surrey, had built stone vaulting over the nearby yew tree, which had a massive 11-metre (36-ft) circumference. This convinced Mr Alan Mitchell, one of Britain's leading experts on trees, that Meredith's ideas were worth taking seriously. 'The fact that the Saxons had had to make foundations to accommodate this tree 1000 years ago made me realize that the yew had been around very much longer than that,' stated Mitchell. Today he says, 'We've more or less agreed that these trees can be more than 4000 years old. In fact, there appears to be no theoretical end to this tree, no reason for it to die.' Yew trees do seem to have the ability to revitalize themselves and some experts have suggested that the species shows no natural signs of ageing. Meredith believes that they could in fact be older than America's giant redwoods and bristlecone pines, currently accepted as the world's oldest tree species.

The yew was an important component of pre-Christian beliefs, but there are also strong associations between Christianity and the yew. The tree is found in many of Britain's churchyards. Indeed, almost all the 400 largest yew trees in the country are situated in church grounds.

Some Christian scholars believe that trees were planted in churchyards because their evergreen foliage was seen as a symbol of everlasting life. Others say that the trees might have been planted to discourage livestock from grazing in the hallowed acre, as the foliage, bark and seeds of the tree are poisonous. But the fact that yews can attain such an age challenges these widely held beliefs. 'This idea that some yews might have been there before the churches themselves turned everything around,' says Alan Mitchell. He now suggests that churches were built near to yews because of the aura of holiness and sanctity that the tree had for the pre-Christian people. In other words, the early beliefs of the Celts and their predecessors were incorporated into Christian practice.

Allen Meredith has found evidence indicating that the association between man and the yew goes back at least to the age of the Celts. Yew trees and oak trees were sacred to the Celtic priests, the druids. They are said to have used tablets of yew wood on which to inscribe

*The Ashbrittle
yew, Somerset*

sacred words in their ogham script. Throughout prehistoric Britain the yew inspired awe and stood out from other vegetation. The Celts believed that the gods lived in its branches. The yew tree was often used as a meeting place, as well as a burial site for important tribesmen. One of the Celtic tribes, the Eburones, took their name from the yew tree: *eburos* means yew in the Celtic language. The word can also be found in the old name for York, which is Eburacum or Eboracum. The etymology of the word yew shows that it has influenced the title of hundreds of places.

The yew tree illustrated on page 57 is at Ashbrittle in Somerset. It is said by Allen Meredith to be 3000 years old, and stands next to a Bronze Age round barrow, which in turn is within an ancient churchyard.

The Gog and Magog oaks

Next we have an account by Brian Lavelle of the oak tree, whose association with the Celts and their elders or priests the druids is legendary. The oak trees illustrated here are a pair a few kilometres east of Glastonbury called Gog and Magog. They are two of the oldest oaks in Britain. (Gog and Magog were mythological figures described in the twelfth century by Geoffrey of Monmouth as 'the last of the British Giants'.)[11]

The extract is taken from Pliny the Elder, the Roman writer (AD 23–79):

> Nothing is more sacred to the druids than the mistletoe and the tree on which it grows, especially if it be an oak. They chose oak woods for their sacred groves, and performed no sacred rite without using oak branches. Whatever grows on the tree is sent from heaven, a sign that the tree has been chosen by the god.'

The oak tree held great importance in the Celtic tradition and prior to that, since prehistoric times. It is a tree specially revered both for its longevity and for its practical use to the community. Oak trees were representatives of the Tree of Life, linking our world with the realms of the Otherworld. The Celts of Continental Europe and Britain held the tree in particular regard.

As to religion, Maximus of Tyre reported that the Celts of Gaul represented Zeus in the form of a high oak tree. The Celtic counterpart to Zeus was Taranis the Thunderer, whose symbols were a spoked wheel, an eagle and a lightning bolt. (The wheel can be seen in the illustration of the Celtic gold 'stater' coin on page 48.) Taranis is also connected to Jupiter and there have been over 150 Jupiter columns found in western Europe, including Cirencester and Chichester. Many of these huge pillars were topped by a statue of a god carrying a spoked wheel and/or lightning bolt. Some are carved with foliage and bark, which has prompted the suggestion that the originals were made of wood, most likely oak trunks. The Germanic and early Celtic peoples are known to have erected great tree trunks in ritual pits such as those at Danebury, where the trunk was some 60 centimetres (two ft) in diameter.

Oak wood was of great importance in other aspects of religion. At the source of the River Seine, an important sacred site, 140 wooden figures were found. The votive offerings ranged from animals and individual limbs to human figures over one metre (three and a half ft) tall. All were of oak wood. At Gristhorpe, near Scarborough, a burial was discovered in an oak coffin, with oak branches and mistletoe carefully laid inside.

The power that oak groves – living temples to the gods – had in the minds of the people and their sanctity are evoked when Lucan describes Julius Caesar cutting down a druidic grove near Marseilles (Massilia): 'The solemnity and terror of the place struck such awe into the labourers that Caesar himself had to seize an axe and drive it into the trunk of an oak, crying, "Believe that I am guilty of the sacrilege and henceforth none of you need to fear to cut down the trees".'

With regard to tribes, the Celtic worship of trees was preserved in both personal, tribal and place-names. Drunemton, meeting place of the Celtic Galatians in Asia Minor, is thought to mean 'the sacred oak grove'. Dergen (Old Welsh) means 'son of the oak', as does Mac Dara in Irish. Druid is believed by some to mean 'wise man of the oak'. Many other tree names abound, such as Mac Ibar and Mac Cuill, son of yew and son of hazel.

Particular oak trees would have been held as sacred, especially solitary or old trees and those found close to springs. Ribbons were tied on to and coins hammered into the venerable giants, as they still are in some places in Ireland, in return for prayers requesting healing or help from the saints.

The importance to the Celts of individual trees led to the appearance in Irish of a word, *bile*, meaning 'sacred tree'. These sacred trees linked the tribes with the Other Realms and were a source of power and pride. Assemblies took place beneath them and raids would have been made in attempts to destroy other tribe's *biles*, thereby humiliating the tribe and damaging their morale. These occasions are mentioned in Irish manuscripts and folklore, and the sanctity of the oak is shown in the Welsh stories from the *Mabinogion*.

In the Seanchus Mor, the ancient law tracts of Ireland, the oak was one of the seven types of Chieftain trees. They were protected with strict penalties and fines for any damage done to them. The chieftain trees were the most important, followed by Peasant, Shrub and Herb trees with lesser fines. The fine for cutting the trunk of the tree was a cow, and a heifer for limbs and branches. One of the reasons for such reverence was the belief that ancestors and other spirits could reside in these trees, thereby strengthening the sense of outrage if they were sacrilegiously damaged.

Regarding everyday use, the importance of the oak tree to the Celts should not be underestimated. Oak timber was used in the construction of sailing ships which were far more durable and superior to those of the Romans. Caesar, speaking of the ships of the Brittany tribes, say:

> The hulls were made entirely of oak to endure any violent shock
> or impact . . . the enemy's ships were better adapted for violent
> storms and other conditions along the coast. They were so
> solidly built that our ships could not damage them with rams . . .
> and if left aground by the tide they had nothing to fear from
> the rocks and reefs. To our ships, on the other hand, all these
> situations were a source of terror.

Oak was also used to construct plank-built houses, and for the support posts of the round houses mentioned earlier (see page 52). It was used as well for pallisades, roads and bridges. The acorns were used to feed pigs, one of the sacred Celtic animals, and the bark was used for tanning leather.

In the Christian era in Ireland in particular, the sanctity of the oak was maintained in place-names, where churches and monasteries were founded close by oak groves. Cille Daire (Kildare) means 'church of the oak', the monastic school at Daire Maugh (Durrow, in Wexford) means 'plain of the oaks', and St Colmcille's favourite church was Daire Calgaich, 'the oak grove of Calgaich'. Groves were also 'de-paganized' by dedicating them to the Virgin Mary, who was given 'Our Lady of the Oaks' as one of her titles.

From all of this, the importance the oak tree at every level of Celtic life can clearly be seen, from the everyday to the myths and religious practices of the society.

During the last decade scientists have been successful in using an extract from the bark of the yew tree, called taxol, to treat some cancers and other major ailments. As this chapter demonstrates, the Celts held sacred all types of trees, and it seems probable that the druids possessed an herbal knowledge which we are only just starting to rediscover today.

SACRED LANDSCAPE SITES AND THEIR CONTINUITY

Our ancestors, from Neolithic times through to the Middle Ages, were attracted to dramatic and unusually shaped natural hills as sites for their rituals and worship. A number of these occur in the south of Britain, where the surrounding land is relatively flat yet due to an unusual geological formation a hill or mound rises from the plains. Indeed, a few of these mounds were entirely man-made, such as the vast site at Silbury Hill in Wiltshire, the largest artificial mound in Western Europe. This striking construction is over 4000 years old.

Other locations started as natural occurrences and then often had additions in the Neolithic or Bronze Age. Probably the best known is Glastonbury Tor in the Vale of Avalon, Somerset, which in Neolithic times and even later would have been an island in the low waters covering the Somerset Levels. This fact still lingers in the name the Isle of Avalon. The Celtic name for Glastonbury was Ynys Wittrin or Isle of Glass. Being such a striking monument, much has been written about this site, including the possibility of there being a prehistoric processional maze leading from the foot of the tor to its summit. Evidence for this is scant, however, and the ridges or terracing are more likely to be the legacy of Iron Age farming practices. Still, the site would have provided a perfect place for observing the rising and setting sun on the seasonal

Glastonbury Tor: 'The Isle of Avalon'

festivals and also the Celtic fire-festivals. St Michael's fourteenth-century chapel on its summit, built over the ruins of an earlier chapel used in connection with the monastic community of Glastonbury Abbey, is an indication that as late as medieval times this site was considered a very sacred place. The earliest evidence of a settlement on the tor dates from the sixth century AD.

Several sites with similar dramatic locations can be found in the West Country, one being near Abbotsbury in Dorset, an area which was well populated by the Celtic Durotriges tribe. The hillside here also has pronounced terracing. Again, whether it was created as a prehistoric processional maze to the summit or is just an example of Iron Age Celtic agricultural terracing is a matter for speculation. No conclusive evidence has come to light for the former. As with Glastonbury, this site would have been perfect for observing the seasonal festivals, having panoramic views in all directions, and Glastonbury Tor and Chapel Hill have many other similarities. Chapel Hill, for example, also has an early medieval chapel on its summit, this one dedicated to St Catherine. The chapel was originally built in connection with the nearby eleventh-century Benedictine monastery of Abbotsbury, whose ruined outline can still be seen on the slope to the north of the vast restored medieval thatched tithe barn.

St Catherine's Chapel, Abbotsbury

Some other hill or 'tor' sites in south-western Britain which have a lengthy continuity of worship culminating in a finely sited medieval chapel are Brent Tor, with its spectacular location on a granite summit on Dartmoor, St Michael's Mount in Cornwall, and Burrow Mump in Somerset.

Burrow Mump is a most unusual site. Some say it is completely man-made; certainly it has been 'structured' by some of its occupants down the centuries. King Alfred fortified it when the area was being besieged by the Vikings, and story of Alfred burning the cakes is said to have occurred here. In the immediate vicinity is the Saxon abbey of Athelney. The sunset photograph overleaf of Burrow Mump was taken after a period of severe winter flooding in the area. It is believed that well before its occupation by Alfred, there was a Romano-Celtic temple on the site.

Burrow Mump, Somerset

The link between many of these hilltop chapels and St Michael is interesting. In recent years the Michael ley line has been evaluated. This runs as a straight line from St Michael's Mount in Cornwall, through Brent Tor (whose chapel is also dedicated to St Michael) on Dartmoor, to St Michael's chapel on Glastonbury Tor, and on through many other Michael-associated churches and chapels, eventually ending on the coast of East Anglia. Ley lines may seem rather hypothetical to some readers, but this one is factually interesting in that on the Celtic festival of Beltane, today's May Day, all the sites on the line are linked by the path of the rising sun. The reader is left to evaluate whether this is 'mere coincidence' or carefully engineered solar alignment by our ancestors.

CELTIC HEAD CARVINGS

To the Celts of the Iron Age in Europe and in Britain before the Roman invasion, the head held a particular significance: it was the seat of the soul, and was therefore held in great reverence. One tradition which may to us sound rather gory but is factual is decapitation. The Iron Age Celts, quite unlike their peaceful and reclusive Celtic Christian monastic descendants, were warfaring tribes who gloried in battle. When another tribe was conquered, the heads of some of the captives were severed and taken back to be displayed on posts outside the conquering tribe's settlement. This was not just seen as an act of strength; the belief was also that the power that had been contained in the head would continue to assist the conquering tribe in their future battles.

In later years, when times became relatively peaceful, the head was still revered and numerous stone carvings have been discovered throughout Europe and Britain of Celtic heads. These have been found 'guarding' sacred places such as wells, springs, temples and shrines. In northern Britain a number of these stone heads have been discovered, some incorporated into later buildings in the area.

Celtic heads may turn up in the most unusual places, and here we have an account of one discovered on Exmoor by local farm-owner Jeffrey Samuel:

The Devonshire farm where we lived was situated in a deep-sided valley which was one of the many which ran up on to Exmoor. The nearest road was one and a half kilometres (one mile) away, and a stream ran along the bottom of the valley with meadows stretching between the base of the hills. In some places the valley was so narrow that it seemed in times gone by it would have dammed itself across, and there would probably have been a lake below where the present farmhouse is. Several of us living there at the time had very real dreams in which the valley was filled with water.

During the 35 years that we lived there I found many interesting stones and flints, which eventually formed a small museum in our barn. Probably the oldest artefact that I unearthed was a stone hand-axe which was dated at 6000 BC.

People took very little interest in these finds and I assumed that they were the kinds of artefact which could be discovered almost any-where. It was only after we left the farm that I discovered this was not so.

One fine sunny day when I was hoeing mangolds in one of the flatter fields at the top of the hill, I was completely amazed to see a stone on which two eyes were carved staring up at me. Picking it up, I could see that there was a face engraved on this quite rough-looking stone, which was little more than five centimetres (two in) across.

The main features apart from the eyes were the nose and mouth, the latter being partly open and showing teeth minutely carved out. It seemed to me that the stone must be very old and must be of great interest, so I was considerably disappointed when I took it to Taunton Museum and was told that it was probably made by an artistically minded farm worker in his dinner-hour, and that it could not be of any great age. The reason they gave for this was that it was made out

The characters of the ogham alphabet (by Anthony Rees)

of poor-quality ironstone, and over time the features would not have survived. They suggested that if I put it in water for a month there would be nothing of the face left. Not wanting to do this with the stone itself, I found one of a similar kind and made a rough carving on it myself.

After I had immersed my own ironstone carving in water for two months there was no change in detail at all. A geologist later commenting on the stone said that it would be quite possible for the markings to survive on the stone for thousands of years if in a fairly dry and stable situation.

Curiosity finally got the better of me and the stone found its way up to the British Museum in London. After careful scrutiny it was classified by Dr Anne Ross as being *c.* AD 300 and almost certainly Celtic in origin.

The stone is now kept in South Molton museum in Devon.

OGHAM SCRIPT

Ogham is an early form of Old Irish and the first known Irish writing. The characters comprise a series of lines and notches which are scored across a long stem-line often on standing stones. In the majority of cases the inscription is read from the bottom up and usually names the person being commemorated, along with their ancestors and the carver of the inscription.

Ogham is often referred to as the Tree Alphabet, because each letter takes the name of a tree. This has led to much speculation that poetry involving trees was used as a means of passing on secret knowledge and messages.

The subject of ogham has always aroused controversy. This is because only secondary textual evidence exists to explain the uses and purpose of ogham writing. Physically the evidence comprises inscriptions on stone pillars and slabs which serve as commemorative memorials and grave markers.

The main textual information comes from the 'Ogham Tract' (Duil Feda) in the Book of Ballymote. Compiled in the fourteenth century, parts are believed to have been copied from an earlier ninth-century text. It contains legends about the origins and uses of ogham, along with descriptions and drawings of extensive variations on the basic ogham alphabet and characters.

Looking at the archaeological evidence, over 350 ogham stones are known, with the majority found in southern Ireland from Kerry to Waterford and in south Leinster. They also occur in small numbers in western Scotland, the Isle of Man and in Cornwall at Lewannick, where Irish settlers from Munster landed and founded communities. While the stones in Ireland are written purely in ogham, those in Britain often have the inscription repeated in Latin carved in Roman characters on the same stone.

The largest concentration of ogham stones outside Ireland is found in Wales – particularly in Dyfed – with a handful in north Wales and Anglesey. Dyfed was settled by the Deisi tribe from Waterford, who

The Ogham

Beithe
Luis
Fearn
Saile
Nuin
Huath
Duir
Tinne
Coll
Quert

Muinn
Cort
Heyetal
Straif
Ruis
Ailm
Ohn
Ur
Edhadh
Ido

brought with them their tradition of carving ogham stones which can be seen at Bridell, Nevern and St Dogmaels, and near the Irish crannog at Llangorse.

Ogham stones are said to date from the third century AD up to the eighth and ninth centuries and many are associated with early Christianity. Frequently they are found in Christian church and burial sites known as cillin, and in some cases crude Christian crosses have been carved into the stone beside the ogham. The tall 'holed' ogham stone illustrated here is from Kilmalkedar churchyard on the Dingle peninsula, County Kerry, Ireland, and dates from around the fourth century AD.

The tradition of carving the ogham stones with Christian crosses may be an amalgamation of earlier pagan customs under the influence of missionaries such as St Ciaran of Saighir and St Declan of Ardmore, who are associated with southern Ireland. Their approach to paganism was less confrontational than that of St Patrick, whose region of influence contains only a scant handful of ogham stones.

The power shift from the Celtic Church to the Church of Rome is likely to have spelled the death knell for ogham as a favoured form of inscription. Some of the stones were dug up and inverted, while many others were removed for use as building material for Christian souterrains. Ireland's ogham stones have frequently been found in these underground tunnels and chambers, where they were used as roofing slabs and support pillars.

Some writers have suggested that ogham may have been in use as early as the first century BC. There is little archaeological evidence to support this claim. However, the dating of the stones is difficult and many were ascribed to the fourth century AD because it was believed that ogham was modelled on the Latin alphabet of that period. Now it is known that a Latin alphabet divided in a similar way to ogham was already in use five centuries earlier in the first century BC. This, combined with the wealth of secondary textual evidence available, supports theories that ogham could have been used in pagan times.

Early ogham inscriptions on grave markers and memorials often contain the name of the deceased's tribe as well as the individual's names, and it is probable that they acted as territorial markers for powerful families and tribes.

'Holed' ogham stone in Kilmalkedar churchyard

THE ADVENT OF CHRISTIANITY

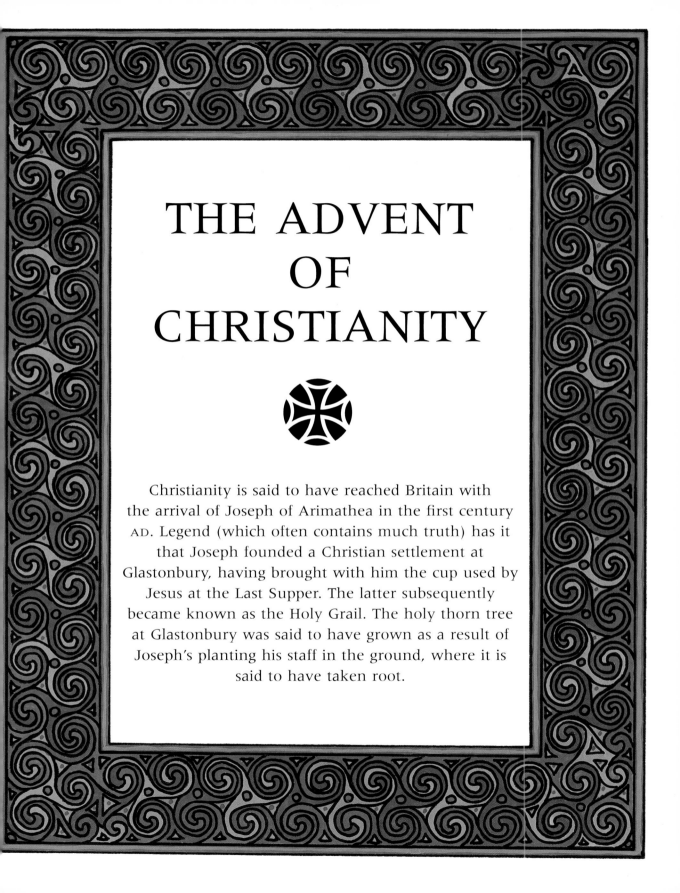

Christianity is said to have reached Britain with the arrival of Joseph of Arimathea in the first century AD. Legend (which often contains much truth) has it that Joseph founded a Christian settlement at Glastonbury, having brought with him the cup used by Jesus at the Last Supper. The latter subsequently became known as the Holy Grail. The holy thorn tree at Glastonbury was said to have grown as a result of Joseph's planting his staff in the ground, where it is said to have taken root.

The initial Christianity which infiltrated Ireland in the fourth century, and subsequently spread to the other Celtic countries via travelling Celtic monks, was not of the Roman variety. Though we lack precise historical evidence, it seems highly likely that the first Christians came directly from the Near East via the tin-trading route to Cornwall. By whatever means they arrived, the Celtic monastic settlements and their beliefs were strongly at variance with those of the Roman Church. Early Celtic Christianity had much more of an affinity with the whole natural world and the seasonal cycles venerated by their predecessors. At the Synod of Whitby in AD 664, when the Celtic and Roman Churches finally came face to face, many of these practices were rejected and prohibited, being changed drastically to suit the customs of the Roman Church. At this point in history many of the original Christian teachings present in Britain and Ireland were forced underground, and are only starting to surface again in this century, thanks to the dedicated work of a few courageous individuals.

PILLAR CROSSES

With the advent of Christianity in Ireland and subsequently Scotland, Wales, Cornwall, the Isle of Man and Brittany, we have the beginnings of the Celtic cross carvings. These started as very powerful and basic pillar carvings, evolving through several hundred years into the great high crosses, regarded by many as some of the finest stone sculptures ever created.

The first pillar crosses have their own unique style and rugged beauty. The designs were carved on to upright standing stones, and it is a matter of debate whether this was a direct progression from the worship of the standing stone from Neolithic times onwards, or whether the incoming Christians felt that they needed to 'de-paganize' the stones by carving their own symbols on them. From the designs it would seem that the former was often the case.

A few of the earliest pillar crosses have the Christian chi-rho symbol (two combined letters of the Greek alphabet, representing the word 'Christos') carved on them. Examples of these exist at Penmachno in Gwynedd and Whithorn in south-west Scotland. The designs on the pillars soon evolved into variations of the Maltese cross, an equi-armed cross within a circle. It is highly unlikely that the symbol at this stage had any relevance to the Crucifixion, being more regarded as a symbol of sacred radiance and light.

A few early pillar crosses from the fourth century AD onwards also have an ogham inscription carved on them, along with decorative patterns more akin to pre-Roman Celtic designs than those of the Christian era. One fine example is at Reask monastic settlement in County Kerry, Ireland, where the spiral designs are carefully carved into the uneven surface of the stone. A line from the spirals ends up encircling the equi-armed cross at the top of the stone. The whole effect is one of great beauty and strength. The letters DNE ('Domine', meaning Lord) are carved vertically on the left-hand side of the stone. The Reask pillar cross dates from the late sixth century AD.

Decorated pillar cross from Reask monastic settlement

For the next 250 years or so, prior to the carving of the great high crosses, carved crosses can be found in all the Celtic countries visited by Irish missionaries. These vary in shape and size, from flat 'slab crosses' carved in high-relief to free-standing crosses of unusual proportions. Sometimes the design was carved to fit the shape of the stone, or perhaps a particularly striking stone was chosen simply for its unusual shape. The early free-standing cross at Cardonagh, County Donegal, Ireland, has a roughly shaped outline with very short, irregularly shaped arms, yet the knotwork design has been carefully carved to fit the irregularities. Another unusual cross was discovered at Riskbuie in Argyll, dating from the late sixth or early seventh century AD, the side arms of which form two spirals and the lower shaft is carved into a primitive fish design. The top arm of the cross is carved into a Celtic-style face. This is seemingly a fusion of early indigenous and Celtic cultures.

The unusual cross illustrated here is in Kilmalkedar churchyard on the Dingle peninsula, County Kerry, Ireland, and is called the Sundial Stone. The Celtic cross carving accurately fits the very unusual 'squared' head, and from its name it was no doubt used at some point in its history as a primitive sundial. The cross dates from the late seventh or early eighth century AD.

The Sundial Stone in Kilmalkedar churchyard

BEEHIVE HUTS

The early Celtic monastic system encouraged monks to travel very widely and, in the steps of their master, to forsake all possessions. Many of these monks were skilled navigators and managed to travel very long distances. In recent years a boat was constructed using materials identical to those used by the Irish monks, and Tim Severin proved that it would have been possible for the monks to have sailed as far as the coast of North America.[12] From the fifth to the tenth centuries AD, many of the Scottish Hebridean islands were inhabited by monks from Ireland. These people were looking for remote wild areas in which to build their little hermitages and live a very basic life dedicated to prayer and the service of the Creator. The dwellings in which they lived, sometimes completely alone, sometimes in small groups or communities, were called beehive huts (or beehive cells), so named because of their visual similarity to the traditional 'bee-skep' or hive. These little stone dwellings were so solidly constructed that a number are still intact today. They can be found from south-west Ireland to the Inner Hebrides, and remains also exist in remote, exposed areas of Wales, Cornwall and Brittany.

One of the most extraordinary locations, and one which also illustrates the dedication and austerity of these Celtic monks, is the cluster of beehive huts on the island of Skellig Michael, 11 kilometres (seven miles) from the south-west coast of Ireland and exposed to the

Celtic hermit's beehive hut on Slea Head

full fury of the Atlantic Ocean. The island is shaped like a small volcano, rising extremely steeply from sea level to a peak of 215 metres (700 ft). There are no trees, and the steps of the hazardous pathway up the side of this precipitous granite rock have been carved by the monks themselves. Perched on a ledge almost 180 metres (600 ft) above a sheer drop to the sea is a stone-walled enclosure containing several well-preserved beehive huts, and a very basic, tall, free-standing cross hewn from a single large stone. Today the idea of anyone living here is almost unbelievable, yet the site was occupied continuously for 250 years. Habitation of Skellig Michael was discontinued after it was raided by marauding Vikings, who killed some of the monks and left the others to starve to death by destroying their boats.

During the time the site was occupied, it is said that the monks brought soil from the mainland over in their small boats and carried it the 180 metres (600 ft) up to their small community, where it was used in a walled compound for growing a few basic vegetables. Today it is hard to imagine this kind of asceticism and the driving force behind it.

There are a few finely preserved examples of beehive huts on the Irish mainland and the one illustrated on page 73 can be found at Slea Head on the Dingle peninsula, County Kerry. It dates from the late sixth or early seventh century AD, having survived over 1300 years of the wild weather associated with the Atlantic coast.

The Sandulf Cross, Kirk Andreas: line drawings of front (below) and reverse (opposite)

ISLE OF MAN CARVINGS

From the fifth century AD onwards, the Isle of Man was also home to Irish Celtic missionaries. Carvings found on the island from this era were purely Celtic, such as the Calf of Man Crucifixion slab. This unique eighth-century sculpture has direct comparisons with Irish metalwork of the same period.

However, by the tenth century the island had been invaded and occupied by the Vikings, whose influence is still much in evidence there today. At this time a unique art form appeared which was created by the Vikings. This incorporated the basic Celtic cross outline, often surrounded with a wheel, and on these stones Celtic knotwork was also used alongside figures from the Norse sagas. Scandinavian runic inscriptions were also widely employed.

Here we have a description of the Sandulf Cross at Kirk Andreas. Kirk Andreas is close to the north end of the island, which is 43 kilometres (27 miles) long and 14 kilometres (9 miles) across at its widest point. The description is by Maureen Costain Richards, a resident born on the island who has spent over 20 years studying, sketching and writing about the Manx crosses:[13]

This cross stands 1.9 metres (six ft four in) high by 38–43 centimetres (15–17 in) wide, and is from 11 centimetres (four and a half in) to 14 centimetres (five and a half in) thick. Each face bears a long-shafted Celtic cross without a circle. The head and arms are plain, with two concentric rings in the centre. The shaft is bordered on the left by a narrow step-pattern, and on the right by a key fret. The centre is a regular 'plait of five'. Above the head of the cross is a horizontal band with a 'plait of four'. Below the foot is another band with ornamented twist and ring double-beaded pattern. Above each arm is a bird; that on the right is a cock, but the one on the left could be a hen or a dove. The spaces at each side of the cross are filled with various beasts, their feet towards the shaft and their heads towards the head of the cross. On the left can be seen a stag chased by a hound. Below this is a square ring-and-buckle design, followed by a man on horseback armed with a club or spear. Then follow two interlaced rings, a boar and a long-horned ox. On the right is a goat, then a wolf with a collar of step pattern round its neck. Following this there is a hound, a hind and a bear. All the animals have spiral ornamentation representing the function of the limbs. The hair or bristles on the animals are shown as short lines.

On the reverse, down the left of the cross shaft is a stag, a knotted serpent, a wolf, a bear, a second wolf and then possibly a third wolf or perhaps a dog. On the right side of the shaft is a goat, followed by a square-looped ring, a ram, a knotted serpent, an ox and a boar. All the animals stand facing the cross. Below is a figure on horseback. At the very bottom of the cross is a hound.

The runic inscription running down the edge of the cross reads, 'Sandulf the Black erected this cross to the memory of Arinbjorg his wife.'

It is very difficult to say who the figures and animals represent on this cross. Possibly they are from the Norse 'horse sagas'. The wolves could be Geri and Freki, who feed at Odin's table. The goat illustrated is possibly Heidrun, who stands above Valhalla, from where the champions get their mead. The boar is Saehrimnir, 'sodden every day and whole again at even'. The carved serpents could refer to Hverqelmir under the roots of Yggdrasil's Ash, where 'so many worms are lying'. The figure on horseback could be Gna, whom Frigg sends into many worlds on errands. She has the horse that runs through air and water, Hofvargr. And lastly the great hound could be Garm.

THE SIGNIFICANCE OF WATER AND HOLY WELLS

Water has been treated as a sacred commodity from time immemorial. It was seen as the life-fluid of Mother Earth and as such was directly connected with the Goddess. Stone Age tribal groups camped or built their villages close to water sources. Lakes, springs, wells and rivers all had their divine guardians, and shrines were made to the god or goddess of that particular region. From Bronze Age times onwards, we know that votive offerings were thrown into lakes, perhaps as supplication to these deities or invocations for the healing of a particular person or the well-being of a tribe.

At Lake Neuchâtel in Switzerland, the centre of the La Tène culture from the fifth century BC onwards, many small artefacts have been excavated from one particular area in conjunction with a wooden platform from which it is believed they were thrown. Again, at lake Llyn Cerrig Bach on Anglesey, north Wales, excavations have revealed a

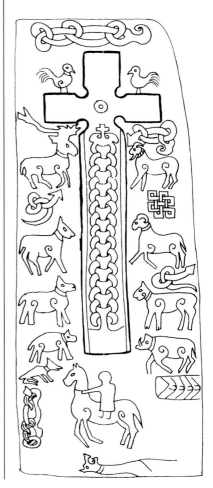

*Iona Abbey,
from the Well of
Healing*

large quantity of artefacts which are believed to have been thrown in for some ritual or ceremonial purpose.

Rivers often were dedicated to aspects of the Goddess. Two examples are the Boyne (see page 18) and the Shannon, whose names are said to originate from the goddesses Boand and Sinann.

The veneration of wells continued from Iron Age times right through to the present day, when many throughout Britain, Ireland and Europe are still visited for their curative properties. The modern custom of tossing a coin into a wishing well to bring good luck is a direct throwback to the veneration of wells and their guardian deities in the Celtic era.

Wells during the Iron Age period of the Celts were often dedicated to aspects of the Goddess, especially Brigit and Anu of the early Irish sagas. The cult of the sacred well was so strong that during the early Christian era these goddesses were adopted by the incoming religion and incorporated into Christianity as St Bridgit (or often St Bride) and St Anne. A number of these wells dedicated to St Bride and St Anne can be found today. Small items such as white quartz pebbles, Goddess figurines and Celtic as well as Roman coins have been discovered at the bottom of some ancient wells.

The healing properties of holy wells have long been known, and from the early Christian era, and no doubt in pagan times before this, folk would travel great distances to drink and sometimes to immerse themselves in the water. Customs such as hanging a small strip of cloth belonging to the afflicted close to the well or throwing in a small object belonging to that person are still followed today in various rural areas, especially in Ireland.

Descriptions follow of three healing wells which have been visited by pilgrims for centuries. These are documented as being much used in the early Celtic Christian era and almost certainly were used for similar purposes hundreds of years before this. First, we have a description of a visit to the Well of Healing on the island of Iona, western Scotland.

This ancient well on the beloved island of Iona occupies a unique position in that it is located close to the summit of Dun I, the highest granite outcrop on the island at just over 90 metres (300 ft). Even in times of drought it is said never to have run dry, despite its exposed location.

Commonly known as the Well of Healing, it was certainly in use during St Columba's life on the island, from AD 563 to 597, and it is dedicated to the saint.

Compared with the other major sites of interest on the island, such as the abbey, the nunnery ruins, the early St Oran's chapel and the renowned Celtic high crosses, the Well of Healing is less widely known, possibly as it is in a more remote spot and entails a steep climb to the top of the island's main granite outcrop in order to find it among the rocks there.

The well itself is a substantial cleft in the rock and the water is very cold, even on a warm summer's day. Tradition has it that pilgrims visiting the island seeking healing would first visit St Columba's monastery, and then make the climb to St Columba's well, where immersion in its water was said to be beneficial for all ailments. Water

St Non (contemporary stained-glass window)

was brought down from the well to the pilgrim if he or she was too infirm to make the journey to the summit.

Undoubtedly the view from the well on a clear day has a powerful effect on both mind and body, as its location is second to none. Standing on the rocks above it and looking north one can see the Isle of Staffa (which inspired Mendelssohn to compose his 'Fingal's Cave' overture). To the east across the Sound of Iona is the rugged coast of the Isle of Mull, with the mountain of Ben More (over 1080 metres/ 3500 ft) outlined powerfully against the sky. In the foreground, almost at one's feet, lies Iona Abbey, the focal point of the island. Looking south-east is the small island of Erraid, while westwards the islands of Coll and Tiree are clearly visible. Tiree receives a greater amount of sunshine than the mainland and, being very fertile compared with Iona, it was used by St Columba's monks to grow wheat for the monastic community.

From the writer's experience, total immersion in the very cold water of the Well of Healing, followed by a brisk towel-down in the sun and wind while taking in the magnificent panorama of the surrounding islands, is a positively exhilarating experience.

In Celtic Christian times, and no doubt with the druids before them who occupied the island prior to the arrival of St Columba (the early Gaelic name for Iona was Innis na Druineach or Isle of the Druids), anyone making a pilgrimage to the Well of Healing would have been undertaking a very special journey, and due to its remoteness it would have been for many a 'once in a lifetime' experience which would remain vividly in their minds for the rest of their lives. The experience hasn't changed for those of us who visit the well today; the whole location is surrounded by an aura of supreme beauty and peace.

A fellow traveller who passed me as I made my way back down the rough granite slope to the abbey smiled at me and said enthusiastically, 'If angels do exist, then I'm sure there are plenty up here!'

I readily agreed.

We next visit St Non's well in Dyfed, south-west Wales. St Non was the mother of St David (d. AD 589), the patron saint of Wales. True to the early Celtic Christian tradition, she too travelled widely and, as depicted in the contemporary stained-glass window illustrated here, made several visits to Brittany, including one with St David. Here follows an account of the well dedicated to her.

St Non's Well, situated on the edge of the Pembrokeshire coast three kilometres (two miles) west of St David's Cathedral, has one of the finest locations of any Celtic healing well. The whole region has a very ancient atmosphere and for the modern-day pilgrim is a most inspiring place to visit. The well has been used for healing purposes at least since the time of St Non, and almost certainly for centuries before that.

St Non was reputed to have given birth to St David close to the well. St David was the founder of the monastery at Menevia in the late sixth century, on the site of today's magnificent St David's cathedral. Both St Non and St David travelled extensively, including journeys to Brittany and Ireland.

Holy wells were an integral part of the belief system of the Celts. At the bottom of some, quartz crystals, white quartz pebbles and even

Roman coins have been found, thrown in as votive offerings to the god or goddess of the well.

The Celts, like any other early civilization, required the basics of food and water around which to build their early settlements. Water was revered, a divine gift from Mother Earth, and the very pure water of wells and springs was considered especially sacred.

Close to St Non's Well, about 460 metres (1500 ft) distant, is the ancient ruined chapel built in the sixth century AD. It is actually constructed within a prehistoric stone circle, a perfect example of convergence and continuance of beliefs. Yet this is hardly surprising as the Scots-Gaelic for 'going to church' is still, when translated, 'going to the stones'. The only carving within the ruined chapel is a fine example of an early slab cross, possibly earlier than the chapel itself. The design is a plain yet powerful equi-armed cross within a circle. Very similar basic cross-designs can be found in Ireland, western Scotland, Cornwall and Brittany.

A few hundred metres south of the ancient chapel is the contemporary chapel of St Non's, built very much on the design of the early Celtic chapel and incorporating many of the ancient stones found in the immediate area. The stained-glass window (illustrated on page 78) is found above the altar in this beautiful little building.

Healing wells are very much 'alive' today, and St Non's Well is still often used for its curative properties, as are a number of other holy wells throughout Britain, Ireland and Europe.

The object of writing about them is not to encourage people to visit them like tourists, but that they should be approached in a spirit of pilgrimage and revered as sacred places. There are many elaborate theories as to how the water is imbued with healing properties. The fact remains that whatever a person's beliefs, the water from holy wells has a beneficial effect on the human body. A number of clergymen today are aware of this, and some hold annual services at the site if there is a holy well in their parish.

From a contemporary scientific point of view, all healing wells tested have been found to contain higher levels of hydrogen peroxide than 'normal' water. Hydrogen peroxide has recently been succesfully used in the treatment of particular cases of cancer, leukaemia and AIDS, as well as many other lesser ailments.

We now journey to a holy well which is familiar to many people, the Chalice Well at Glastonbury in Somerset. Here follows a description of this ancient sacred place.

Much legend surrounds the beautiful Chalice Well at Glastonbury. As mentioned earlier (see page 69), it is said that Joseph of Arimathea settled in Glastonbury during the first century AD and founded the first Christian settlement here. The chalice of the Last Supper that he is supposed to have brought with him gives its name to the holy well.

If the legend about Joseph's community is correct, then the obvious place for it would have been in the vicinity of Chalice Well, which is the main natural water source in the area. The well itself has an output of 120,000 litres (25,000 gallons) a day, and the water has a very high iron content, giving rise to the brownish-red encrustation of the stones over which it has flowed for many an age. To give an idea of its importance, in the drought of 1921–2, the well was the sole provider of fresh water for the entire town.

Little has been carried out in the way of archaeological excavation, and rightly so, due to the beautiful peaceful setting of the present-day Chalice Well gardens, which are visited by many thousands of people every year. The finds that have been made, however, are very significant.

In a trench about four metres (12 ft) below the level of the present well, the substantial root of a yew tree was unearthed. After accurate examination by Leeds University the tree was pronounced to have been alive from *c.* AD 300, and together with the fact that its remains are in a straight line with other living yew trees further down the gardens, this indicates that there may well have been a sacred pathway to the well in very early times. This would be in accord with the Celtic reverence for both the yew tree (see also pages 55–8) and the well itself.

It is believed that at the time when this yew tree was alive, the well was a prolific natural spring emerging directly from the ground at a point lower than the present-day well.

The well dates from two different periods. The shaft is from the mid-twelfth century and is built of stone taken from the early Glastonbury Abbey, which was destroyed by fire in 1184. Then from excavations of wooden conduits it is thought that the well supplied the later abbey in the mid-thirteenth century.

Connected to the well-shaft is a pentagonal stone chamber, built during the eighteenth and nineteenth centuries, which is thought to have acted as a 'water purifier', before the water travelled downhill to the pilgrim's bathing pool in the gardens and the pump room in the town itself.

Today the well has a fine wooden lid with a wrought-iron design known as 'Vesica Pisces'. This is a very ancient symbol which was later adopted by Christians as the central oval resembles the Sacred Fish. The well-cover was given as a peace offering by friends and admirers of the Chalice Well and its environment in 1919, and was blessed in that year by the Archdeacon of Wells Cathedral.

Also in the trench mentioned earlier, where the yew tree root was discovered, several flint tools were found from the Palaeolithic era (remnants of a Goddess-centred habitation close to the spring?), as well as an Iron Age pottery shard. Subsequent layers revealed Roman and medieval pottery.

The actual 'fame' of the well did not become widespread until the mid-1700s, when a Somerset man published an account of an unusual dream he had had in which he was instructed to drink the well's water for seven successive Sundays. This he did, and found that his chronic asthma was cured immediately. Thereafter many thousands of people flocked to the small town, and soon a 'book of cures' was compiled, with official testimonies recorded as to the authenticity of each.

Today the well is still visited by many people who come to drink the water for its curative properties, or to replenish themselves in the peaceful garden surroundings. The water nowadays flows underground from the well itself, emerging at the sculpted lion's head set into a low wall further down in the gardens. It is here that one is recommended to drink the crystal-clear water.

*The Chalice Well
at Glastonbury*

THE PICTS AND THEIR LEGACY

The origins of the Picts are still something of a mystery to present-day historians. That they were the inhabitants of eastern and northern Scotland from at least the time of the Roman invasion of Britain is certain, but their culture did not begin solely with the advent of Celtic tribes in this region. Their language is known to have been a mixture of Celtic words along with an earlier 'lost' language, possibly originating from the Bronze Age inhabitants of this region before them.

They were established as a kingdom at the time of St Columba, and are mentioned in the seventh-century *Life of St Columba*, written by the monk Adamnan. Columba ventured into the land of the Picts to introduce their king to Christianity. (It was also on this journey that he made his legendary acquaintance with 'Nessie', the Loch Ness monster.)

Very little historical writing exists about the Picts. One rather amusing description from a twelfth-century Icelandic text describes them as 'small men who did wonders in the mornings and evenings, but who at midday lost their strength and had to hide away underground'.

The legacy the Picts have left us is their magnificent stone carvings. In AD 843 the Scottish and the Pictish kingdoms were united, which promoted a cultural flow between the two regions.

Pictish carvings, with their strange symbols combined often with elaborate Celtic knotwork, spirals and key-patterning, have a beauty all of their own. Technically they have been divided into three classes of stone. 'Class 1' stones are carved with purely Pictish symbols and date mainly from the seventh century AD. 'Class II' stones contain elaborate knotwork Celtic crosses surrounded by Pictish carvings and date from the mid-eighth to the mid-ninth century AD. 'Class III' Pictish stones are those from this region devoid of Pictish symbols and consisting solely of Celtic crosses and designs.[14]

To convey some of the true flavour of the Pictish carvings we have this description of their mystery by James Gillon-Fergusson, a sculptor who was born and brought up in southern Pictland. He has made a detailed study of these carvings, culminating in the creation of miniature facsimiles of many of the stones with their amazingly intricate detail.

The Hilton of Cadboll Pictish stone (facsimile reproduction in miniature by James Gillon-Fergusson)

In Angus, an ancient area of southern Pictland, there are many Pictish stone carvings, some of which still feature prominently in the landscape. It was near these sacred places that I grew up and as a child became fascinated by the mystery of these lonely monuments carved by Pictish sculptors over 1000 years ago.

Their tradition of stone carving was assisted by a good supply of sandstone found on the east coast of Scotland, the raw material into which they carved their fine detail. Many of these surviving examples of Pictish art are carved in the distinctive and unusual format of cross slabs, creating a solid and imposing form, in addition to which the Pictish sculptor carved strange and mysterious symbols. These stones capture modern imagination and provoke thoughts of wonder about a unique culture, their forgotten ways and lost language. Thoughts perhaps turn to why the Pictish culture died out, rather than being passed down from generation to generation.

A few years ago when I had time on my hands, I made many pilgrimages to the well-known group of Pictish stones at Aberlemno in Angus, where some stones still stand in their intended position in the landscape and have another dimension of presence. Captivated by their imagery and finding myself absorbed by those thoughts of wonder, I began to convince myself that I could relate the same impact of the complex patterns and something of their sense of mystery in miniature.

I chose for my first subject the Kirkton of Aberlemno Battle Stone, which had captured my imagination and was my obvious choice for many reasons. It is one of the most distinctive Pictish stones, tapering from the bottom upwards towards the apex, with similar angles to a pitched roof creating a distinctive outline. The cross boldly projects beyond the surrounding panels, creating a further dimension to the form of the stone, while being covered in the various disciplines of Celtic art: knotwork, spirals and key patterns. The surrounding panels are inhabited by curious entwined animals, while on the other side of the stone is a unique depiction of the Battle of Dunnichen in AD 685 (an important victory for the Picts over their Northumbrian agressors), offering historical insight into the Picts and enough inspiration to begin the miniature stone.

Pictish slab cross from Inchnabraoch (facsimile reproduction in miniature by James Gillon-Fergusson)

Having chosen a technically ambitious stone, I spent as much time as possible with a variety of tools on sample pieces as I did carving the subject. In time the necessary skills grew, and the various patterns which at first seemed infinite became an addictive challenge. During the carving of the 20-centimetre (eight-in) miniature I gradually acquired a variety of tools which would be familiar to any dental technician, enabling accurate rendition of detail in the more intricate sections of knotwork, and later on to shape character into the more textural and rough appearance of the Pictish stones. When I initially finished my first stone, a great feeling of accomplishment was reward enough for those hours of patience.

My enthusiasm for these magnificent carvings led me to create more including the three stones illustrated on pages 82, 83 and here. They are all 'Class II' Pictish stones (see page 82). The Hilton of Cadboll Stone, one of the finest, was originally discovered in Ross-shire and is now in the National Museum of Scotland. It dates from the eighth or early ninth century AD. Of a very similar date are the Meigle cross slab from Meigle in Perthshire (illustrated here) and the Pictish cross slab from Inchnabraoch in Forfarshire.

During my subsequent years as a sculptor it has been very rewarding to see a widespread interest in this once neglected subject which is such an integral part of Scotland's heritage.

The Meigle cross slab (facsimile reproduction in miniature by James Gillon-Fergusson)

Two further examples of Pictish carvings follow. The Sueno Stone is the largest of all the Pictish stones, and its description here is by Geoff Pattison, a lecturer in Fine Art at the University of Northumbria:

> The trip to Forres in Morayshire to see the Sueno Stone is part of my continual quest to find any relative associations with my main concern, the Lindisfarne Gospels book.
>
> However, I had joined that resolute association The Pictish Arts Society, and armed with Anthony Jackson's *The Pictish Trail*, I set off from Cumbria the day after seeing what I believed was appropriate, the beautiful Gosforth Cross, with its Viking and Christian carved symbolism.
>
> Like all journeys, you don't take a journey, it takes you. The journey to a place is often as important as arriving there, and in a strange way you know instinctively when it is time to leave. There is a car park now for visitors to this, the largest of the Pictish stones, which is nearly six metres (20 ft) in height and was carved in the ninth century AD. In some way the time and approach to this monument are important; it is a matter not only of respect but of relative human scale.
>
> The Sueno Stone is now housed in a huge glass case protecting it from all eventualities, including the weather, and in this way achieves a superior air of sculptural respect. However, what is interesting, as the monument stands next to a housing estate, it has defined the dignity of its own space, approachable yet untouchable. It is now within its own 'vacuum', encased like a grand obelisk within its own pyramid, its own time, its own mystery. (The illustration here predates the stone's encasement.)
>
> The Sueno Stone is a 'Class III' stone in Pictish reference in the sense that it is a dressed stone with a Christian cross but no Pictish symbols as such. The Northumbrian links to Pictish territory are well known, but what I find fascinating, as Isabel Henderson discusses in the booklet 'Rosmarkie's Pictish Monuments',[15] are the possible comparisons between the 'pinhole and grid' folios of the Lindisfarne Gospels and those of the constructional and proportional guide lines of Viking sculpture.
>
> As the Pictish stones were in all probability painted – and various scholars have put forward this probability for many of the Celtic high crosses also – is there any parallel between these stones and the illuminated 'cross-carpet' pages of the Lindisfarne Gospels? Has the Sueno Stone become in my mind like a huge illuminated painting?
>
> To describe the content or subject of the Sueno Stone is to open up the debate. One theory is that the monument was erected for reasons of power – one system dominating another. The stone is not a symbolic message *by* the Picts but in fact *for* the Picts, as a continuous reminder of the power and authority of the Scottic force led by Kenneth MacAlpin, who eventually destroyed and obliterated the Pictish state and culture.
>
> If this is true, then the Sueno Stone stands like the Duke of Sutherland over the Highland Clearances. Or is it not similar to that famous painting by David Morier of the Battle of Culloden, done for the Duke of Cumberland, in which the artist used Scots prisoners taken after battle for his models – perhaps the ultimate in humiliation?

The Sueno Stone

The Picts disappeared in a similar way to the highland clans, another irony for Kenneth MacAlpin.

Inverness and Culloden are only 40 minutes from Forres, and so two monuments of resolution and destruction stand in close proximity. Perhaps the Sueno Stone and Culloden have more in common than we realize.

The final Pictish carving in this section is the Glamis Manse Cross, most unusual in that it represents the transition from 'Class I' to 'Class II' Pictish carvings. The cross dates from the early eighth century AD. This description is by Marianna Lines, a Scottish resident who has spent much of her life studying, drawing and writing about Pictish carvings:[16]

The Glamis Cross, Forfarshire, Scotland

The early history of Glamis begins romantically with a cave and a saint. St Fergus of Glamis was a Celtic visionary who lived in the seventh century AD and came to Glamis late in his life, after spending many years travelling in Ireland and Scotland. He was known as Fergus Cruithnech, a Pict, and was Bishop of Scotia (Ireland). As head of a small community in Angus, he is said to have lived in a cave in the Den of Glamis and to have conducted his worship at the well which bears his name today. He died at Glamis and his head was taken to the Abbey of Scone as a sacred relic. Thereafter, the majestic carved stone cross was raised in his honour in Glamis churchyard. This is the legend of St Fergus of Glamis and the basis of our inheritance today in the pleasant valley of Strathmore.

The present church at Glamis is dedicated to St Fergus and considers its foundations to be the original holy well. The great Pictish cross slab in the manse gardens at Glamis is magnificent, and although it is generally dated to the early eighth century AD by experts, there is no reason to believe that it could not have been erected to venerate the saint at a later date.

This great relic of Pictish power can tell more about this sacred site of royal domain. The cross slab at Glamis is thought to be in its original position, somewhat rare nowadays for Pictish stones, the reason being that the manse gardens would originally have been part of a larger churchyard around the church. The orientation is east–west, in a direct axis with the present eighteenth-century church, which is built on the foundations of the medieval 'kirk' dating from 1292. Part of the medieval building can still be seen in the atmospheric Strathmore aisle.

The prominent great relief cross on the front or east face of the stone also represents the four directions – a symbol as significant to the early people of the time as the cross became to the converted Picts. The stone is possibly the most important Pictish symbol stone of all, for it marks a transition from 'Class I' to 'Class II' stones, bearing both early incised and relief style carving. The east face is undressed, and cleverly carved with pre-Christian pagan symbols of the serpent, salmon and mirror, within the natural contours of the stone. The symbols and myths of many Celtic cultures are integrated on the cross slab face. A 'sermon in stone' beyond them all, the Glamis stone's symbolism takes one through the conversion process to a deep under-standing of the nature-oriented beliefs of the Christians living in Britain only 800 years after the birth of Christ.

The important fact is that these Christian and pagan symbols could rest so comfortably together on the same stone. The use of symbols certainly began in pagan times, perhaps as pictograms of their cos-mology, but they were not considered to be in conflict with the Christian message. The cross and the symbols remained integral in the design of these great stone slabs for a period of at least a century.

The symbols on the earlier incised face, the serpent, the salmon and the mirror, are all symbols of fertility and earth wisdom. The serpent is a naturalistic representation of the common adder, as well as being a universal native symbol of regeneration and transfiguration. The salmon is naturally the king of the waters and a symbol of wisdom from Celtic mythology, in addition to its strong power as the earliest Christian symbol. Some also see these iconographic symbols as having heraldic importance, in that the totemic symbol of the salmon, for example, would have been identified with a certain tribe. This type of ancient badge was surely the predecessor of the clan heraldry system.

The cross-face presents four primal images around the heavily interlaced cross pattern. Top left is a Pictish lion as seen in the Book of Durrow, the symbol of St Mark. Top right is a centaur waving double axes, a symbol of the dual nature of man as part-animal, and the struggle between spirit and flesh. The lower left panel shows a pair of Pictish warriors in battle below the image of a boiling cauldron, pairs of legs kicking out of the top – a symbol of rebirth if related to the famous Taliesin of Welsh folklore; or perhaps of foreboding, since the Picts are said to have practised execution by drowning.

This panel is balanced by the direct Pictish symbols of the deer head (the deer being the symbol of the soul 'thirsting for the waters of life', as well as the essence of the spirit of nature at peace in the wild) and the cauldron, shown in plain form, symbolizing the chalice of life and cup of plenty in the Celtic/Pictish world.

The entire sculpted stone face is wrapped with an encircling pair of animals in the contemporary manuscript illumination style of zoo-morphic interlace, whose heads meet at the top of the stone, although the motif is barely visible today. The original hand of the sculptor who created this stone of unique carving is seen in every line of the design, down to the tapered triangular shape of the stone as a whole.

Meditation, as befits the venerable St Fergus of Glamis, can still be practised by the modern pilgrim who gazes on this stone.

THE CELTIC HIGH CROSS

When speaking of the Celts, one of the most evocative images that springs to mind is the Celtic cross. From Cornwall to the Isle of Man, from Wales to the Hebrides and throughout Ireland, many magnificent examples of free-standing carved Celtic crosses can be found, some of which are at least 1200 years old.

Contemporary carved crosses almost invariably signify a burial place, yet the early free-standing or high crosses were not erected for this purpose. The majority were positioned as meeting places, often within a Celtic monastic settlement, and were carved for the sheer enjoyment of creating beauty, or 'to the Glory of God'. As well as biblical scenes, many have knotwork patterns, spirals, mythical beasts and raised bosses, the latter said by some to symbolize the sun, worshipped by the early Celts.

Some of the early free-standing crosses were completely devoid of design, yet they possess a dignity and power, often enhanced by their location and bold outline.

We will start our journey to some of the ancient high crosses with a visit to the sacred island of Iona, in the Inner Hebrides. This tiny island is known as 'The Mecca of the Gael', and it is said that before the island was invaded by the Vikings, from the seventh century AD onwards, there were over 300 Celtic crosses here. The Vikings destroyed almost all of these, throwing them into the Sound of Iona, the narrow strip of water which separates Iona from the Isle of Mull.

On this wondrous island today there are three free-standing crosses. St Martin's Cross (illustrated on page 106) is a magnificent example of stone sculpture. It stands to the south of Iona Abbey, overlooking the Sound of Iona, most probably still in its original position. It measures over five metres (17 ft) high and is carved from a very hard volcanic stone, Lewissian gneiss. There are slots in the ends of the arms which are believed to have housed wooden extensions, thus enlarging the proportions of the cross on particular festival days. The cross itself has been dated to the ninth century AD. The intricate carving on the front depicts various biblical scenes, while the back is elaborately carved with 'boss-and-serpent' designs, hinting at a synthesis with earlier pagan worship on the island (as we have already seen) – one of the island's Gaelic names is Innis na Druineach or Isle of the Druids.

The original Celtic Christian community on the island was founded by St Columba (or Columcille in Gaelic) in AD 563. There are a few remains of beehive huts on the island dating from this time, including one known as 'the hermit's cell', supposed to have been used by Columba himself.

Two other beautiful free-standing Celtic crosses can be seen on the island. One is St John's Cross, illustrated on page 90, which stands outside the west door of the abbey. The original cross dates from the late eighth century AD, and the present cross is a cast from it, as the original was taken several years ago to the mainland for preservation and restoration. I recall, when living on the island in the early 1960s and working for the Iona Community, that the top section of the original was kept in a wooden chest behind the Abbey Museum. Having asked permission, together with a friend I was allowed very carefully to 'unpack' the sections and piece them together on the grass behind the abbey. Seeing the original eighth-century cross head lying there complete on the grass was a most memorable experience. St John's Cross is one of the most delicately carved of any of the Celtic crosses; it is believed that the Kildalton Cross on the Isle of Islay was carved by the same school of stonemasons.

The third standing Celtic cross on the island, illustrated here, is of a later date than the other two, probably from the fourteenth century. It is known as MacLean's Cross and can be seen on the left-hand side of the roadway as one walks from the jetty to the abbey. It is what is known as a disc-headed crucifixion cross, having a carving of the Crucifixion in the centre of the round head, which is unpierced, as in the earlier crosses. The cross is tall and very slender, with panels of intricate interlacing meticulously carved right down the shaft. Parallels can be made with other crosses of this period, such as the Oronsay Priory Cross on the island of Oronsay, and a number of similarly styled Crucifixion crosses in southern Ireland.

The museum on Iona contains various earlier basic slab crosses, as well as two fine Norse carvings depicting Viking ships and with runic inscriptions. There is also a further carved cross shaft among the various carvings.

The magnificent island setting for these Celtic crosses is idyllic, and anyone who has visited Iona will carry the experience with them for the rest of their lives.

MacLean's Cross, Iona

St John's Cross,
Iona

While still in western Scotland the next Celtic high cross we visit is on the beautiful Isle of Islay, reached today by ferry from Tarbert at the north end of the Kintyre peninsula. Here follows an account by Christopher Tweedale of a recent visit to some of the ancient sites on the island, including the beautifully carved Kildalton Cross.

The island of Islay must surely rank as one of the most important sites for those with a love of Celtic/megalithic/early Christian lore. Islay lies 22 kilometres (14 miles) west of the Kintyre peninsula. It has standing in its original site the best-preserved early Celtic wheel cross in the British Isles outside Eire. This is at Kildalton and dates from around AD 800.

The island has many examples of stone carvings from this period and later which are well documented.

The Kildalton Cross, Islay

Ignoring the whisky distilleries (if you can!), the island had a definite aura of mystique. We visited in September and particularly noticed the vividness of the autumnal colours there, the relatively unspoilt coastline and abundant wildlife. We found it easier to imagine the Celtic holy men landing at Islay than Iona. In fact, tradition has it that St Columba's tutor in Ireland, namely St Ciaran, established himself at Kilchiaran in the Rinns of Islay on the Atlantic coast, and that he died here in AD 548.

Most especially we felt that the early Celtic religious settlement of Kilnave retains much of the original atmosphere, the peace and tranquillity of its conception. The once beautiful but now very weathered high cross, dated at *c.* AD 850 and 2.6 metres (eight ft six in) high, in the chapel grounds of Kilnave on the edge of the sea loch Loch Gruinart, although not in such pristine condition as the cross at Kildalton, is important in its own right, as the barely discernible carvings on it bear a direct resemblance to those on the high cross at Kells in County Meath, Ireland. The carving on the lower shaft is very reminiscent of the La Tène artistic style. The name Kilnave means Church of the Saints. This is a very lonely place.

Kilchoman, which is also on the Atlantic coast, a mere three kilometres (two miles) north of Kilchiaran, has a beautiful free-standing disc-headed cross, albeit of a much later date (late fourteenth to early fifteenth century) standing among many elaborately carved grave slabs. There is also a broken floreated disc-headed cross, the Mac-Innirlegin Cross, named after the head of the monastic school there which flourished *c.* 1480.

Interestingly, most of the early chapels are intimately associated with standing stones – naturally so, for they are very potent points of earth energy.

There is a wealth of megalithic remains on Islay, and some of the standing stones are huge, especially in the Port Ellen area. Unfortunately, the burial chambers are very ruinous, yet this in our opinion makes them very old. As in many other parts of Britain, some standing stones have been Christianized, or rather de-paganized, by having Christian symbols carved on them.

Continuing our tour of Islay, five kilometres (three miles) south of Port Charlotte we arrive at Nereabolls, a ruined chapel and burial ground containing some of the finest medieval carved grave slabs in Scotland, and second only to Saddell Abbey on the Kintyre peninsula, which has relief grave slabs depicting armed knights.

There is to be mentioned one further gem of Islay's history, and that is Finlaggan. Here on a tiny island in Loch Finlaggan was held for hundreds of years the court of the Lords of the Isles. (A recent *Time Team* BBC television programme on archaeological investigation, presented by Tony Robinson, gave an excellent and detailed account of this site.) The Clan Donald chiefs bore the title 'Lords of the Isles', and British royalty continues the tradition even today.

However, the glory of Islay is the Kildalton Cross. It is approached by a narrow road hugging the coast, through woodland which goes down to the sea, past basking seals, everywhere quiet and still. Interestingly, a small stone on which is carved a Latin cross was found buried below it.

Carved from a single block of local bluestone, the Kildalton

Cross stands 2.7 metres (nine ft) high and is a masterpiece of Celtic sculpture. It is very likely that it was originally painted in bright colours, and this suggestion, connected with the colours of the great illuminated Gospels, has been put forward with regard to many of the Irish high crosses. About half-way up on the reverse side is what has been described in the past as the mysterious 'nest of eggs' symbol, carved in very high relief. This symbol also appears a number of times on St John's Cross on Iona (see page 90). Interpretations range from its being a symbol of the Holy Trinity to a symbol of druidic sun/nature worship. Its true meaning is open to speculation. The Kildalton Cross is one of the wonders of early Celtic stone-carving.

Mysteries abound on the Isle of Islay. Despite recent excavations and research there are many secrets yet to be discovered.

Our pilgrimage to some of the great Celtic crosses now takes us to Wales, where we have accounts of two of the most imposing of these beautiful monuments. The first is the Great Cross at Nevern, in Dyfed, and here follows a description of the area in which the cross is found:

Nevern, or Nanhyver as it was known in early Celtic times, must be one of the most interesting Celtic sites in Wales. The ancient church stands in a wooded valley a few kilometres from Cardigan, on the south-west coast of Dyfed. It is dedicated to St Brynach, an Irish-born Celtic monk, who married the daughter of a Breconshire chieftain and subsequently established a number of chapels in the area, of which Nanhyver was the principal. He died in AD 570 and was thus a contemporary of St David. There is a text in the British Library entitled *The Life of St Brynach*, written not long after his death.

As you enter the church gates, the path leads down an avenue of ancient yew trees said to date from about the fifth century AD. At the end of the avenue, sheltered close to the church wall, stands Nevern Great Cross, illustrated here. This is probably the finest high cross in Wales, and was carved about AD 1000.

It is very well preserved and is decorated with panels of knotwork and chevron designs. The head of the cross is carved separately and is very graceful, with an interlaced pattern surrounding it. The front and the reverse of the cross have different designs, as do the two sides, and the monument is a visual delight for those interested in Celtic carvings.

Within the church is the Maglocunus Stone, a bilingual stone of much value to those interested in the early Celts, as it is one of the few existing stones with inscriptions in both Latin and ogham script.

There is also a very early Celtic slab cross in the church with an unusual design, probably a basic representation of the human form. It has crudely interlaced arms, head and 'legs'. This stone dates from the sixth century AD. Nevern was on the Pilgrims' Route to St David's, one of the most revered places of pilgrimage in Britain. To give an idea of its sanctity in the Middle Ages, two pilgrimages from Canterbury to St David's were held as being equivalent to one pilgrimage to the Holy City of Rome.

It is worth bearing in mind that we are very fortunate in having such a wealth of Celtic interest to experience at Nevern, and in the light of this we should approach the site with reverence.

Nevern Great Cross, Dyfed

The Carew Cross, Dyfed

We travel on to another high cross in Wales, also in Dyfed. This is located today close to the junction of the Saundersfoot–Pembroke docks road and the A4075 northbound route.

The Carew Cross stands approximately four metres (13 ft) high and dates from the ninth century AD. There are finely preserved panels of knotwork and key-patterning on both the east and the west faces of the cross. On the west face there is an inscription to Maredudd ap Edwin, ruler of this region of Dyfed from 1033 to 1035. This inscription was almost certainly added at a later date, as with the fine Houelt Cross at Llantwit Major, which also has a royal inscription.

The cross is close to the hauntingly atmospheric ruins of the early medieval Carew Castle, a fascinating yet somehow unnerving edifice with a very chequered history.

The Carew Cross may well have had a small adjoining chapel, but today no remains are visible. To view the east side of the cross, it is necessary to stand flattened against the hedge of a very fast main road (to avoid in turn being flattened by passing lorries!). This illustration of the west face is a composite of four separate pictures, as it is impossible, due to its positioning in a deep alcove, to encompass the western side fully even with a good wide-angle lens.

This is a fine example of one of the few free-standing high crosses in Wales and well worth a visit, bearing in mind that the fortunate medieval pilgrim would have been making his way across open countryside, without having to encounter the hazards of twentieth-century motor traffic.

Continuing our pilgrimage we now travel to Monasterboice in County Louth, Ireland, to visit the Cross of Muiredach, one of the most beautiful of the Irish high crosses still standing. The early Celtic settlement of Monasterboice, which also contains a fine round tower, is about eight kilometres (five miles) north-west of the town of Drogheda and 13 kilometres (eight miles) inland from the east coast of Ireland. It is also close to the estuary of the sacred River Boyne, and Newgrange chambered cairn (see pages 17–21) is only a few kilometres south-west of this major Celtic monastic site. The following description of the cross is given by Claire Clancy, a resident of the area:

The Cross of Muiredach is one of the finest of the Irish high crosses still standing, and is covered with intricate and detailed sculpted work. It is also extremely well preserved. At the base on the west side can still be seen the inscription in Irish 'OR DO MUIREDACH LASNDERNAD IN CHROS', which when translated means, 'A prayer for Muiredach for whom this cross was made'. Most scholars think this applies to Muiredach, son of Domhnaill, an abbot of Monasterboice, who died *c.* AD 922.

The main sculpture on the circular head of the west side is an elaborate Crucifixion scene, while on the eastern side there is an even more interesing and elaborate Last Judgement. The faces of the shafts on the wide sides show incidents from the life of Christ, incidents from the Old Testament, stories from the lives of the saints and symbolic figures, while the sides of the shafts, the arms and ring and top of the shaft are all richly sculptured, some with the most unusual and fantastic animals and birds, in addition to the usual intricate Celtic ornamentation.

However, the scenes on the high cross are not confined to just religious and biblical subjects, and there are several which are open to interpretation.

The scenes on the shaft of the cross are to be read from the bottom up. In the accepted enumeration, the three scenes on the west shaft are numbered 21, 22 and 23. These are said to represent Christ seized in the Garden, the incredulity of Thomas (where Thomas is said to be thrusting his hands into Christ's side) and Christ seated between Peter and Paul, giving the keys to one and the book of the Gospels to the other.

A very different interpretation has recently been suggested by several scholars. This interpretation sees panel 21 as representing two Viking soldiers and suggests that the central figure is the Celtic abbot whom they are seizing roughly. In panel 22 the same two men

The Cross of Muiredach, Monasterboice

with their Viking moustaches are shown, but now they are wearing ecclesiastical robes, while the central figure, clean-shaven and with a coronal tonsure as before, has his hand raised in blessing. In panel 23 all three ecclesiastics are wearing Viking moustaches, and they have the keys and the book of the Gospels. Those who have interpreted the panels in this manner say that they tell the story of the encounter of the abbot with the Viking invaders, the latter's eventual conversion to Christianity and indeed acceptance as monks at Monasterboice, and finally the time when one of their number became abbot of the monastery.

The Lonan Cross, Isle of Man

There is some historic support for this interpretation. One of the first permanent Viking settlements, a fortified stronghold, was made 13 kilometres (eight miles) from Monasterboice at Annagassan on the Louth coast in AD 840. It is recorded that from there the Vikings plundered Clonmacnoise to the west in AD 841 and Armagh to the north in AD 850. Yet Monasterboice, only a couple of hours' march away, was never plundered by them. They remained at Annagassan until AD 925 and must have had contact with the monastery. If indeed some of their number were converted to Christianity and then became monks, then Monasterboice's immunity from attack is explained.

Are these panels then direct representations of biblical scenes or are they depictions of actual events occurring a short time before the high cross was sculpted? We may never know for sure, but the depiction of the Viking moustaches is suggestive of factual events around Monasterboice in the ninth century AD.

The site of the Muiredach Cross is peaceful and inspiring, and anyone with an interest in exquisite Celtic stone carving will experience great delight and wonder from beholding this magnificent high cross.

From Ireland, we travel as the seafaring fifth- and sixth-century Celtic monks did to the Isle of Man. On the east side of the island, close to the remains of Lonan Old Church and overlooking Laxey Bay, stands the Lonan Cross. This fine and sturdy cross with its elaborate Celtic knotwork dates from the ninth or early tenth century AD, and is said to be the only early cross on the island which still stands in its original site. The following description is by Harold Costain Richards.

The large, disc-headed cross leans at an angle. The outline on the front face is of an equi-armed Celtic or wheel cross with very elaborate knotwork filling the entire space. Every conceivable area of the cross head is filled with detailed interlace patterning, including the recessed ring within the high-relief wheel. Below the cross design are four separate strands of plaiting with differing designs, adding to the beautiful and complex patterning of the cross. Strangely, the reverse side is plain 'faced' stone and completely undecorated.

The cross is set into its own plinth and in shape is most unusual and impressive. The overall height is 2.6 metres (eight ft five in), yet the width of the disc is over 90 centimetres (three ft). It has an almost even thickness throughout of only ten centimetres (four in). Unlike most of the free-standing crosses on the island, this one would have been carved before the Viking invasion and retains its purely Celtic characteristics. It is a magnificent work of Celtic carving and anyone visiting the island is recommended to make a pilgrimage to this site.

Our last port of call on this pilgrimage is to Cornwall. A number of free-standing crosses can be found here, rather shorter and stockier in outline than their Welsh, Scottish and Irish counterparts. Two of the finest decorated Cornish Celtic crosses are the Cardinham Wheel Cross, which dates from the eighth or early ninth century AD, and the Lanherne Crucifixion cross, with its interlacing patterning and dedication to one 'Runhol' (possibly the sculptor himself), which now stands outside Lanherne Convent. The latter dates from the tenth century AD.

The cross we will consider is the impressive 'holed' cross of St Piran near Perranporth.

Much interesting legend surrounds this beautiful early free-standing Celtic cross. Its precise date is uncertain but it is mentioned in a charter written in AD 960, and is believed to have been carved considerably earlier than this.

St Piran himself was a Welsh monk of Irish descent. Like a number of his adventurous contemporaries, he crossed the Bristol Channel in a light boat, subsequently travelling widely in Cornwall before establishing a hermitage at Perranporth. Legend has it that he miraculously crossed the Bristol Channel on a millstone – probably this involves a bit of the Celtic art of 'story-telling' and the original episode has been

St Piran's Cross, near Perran-porth, Cornwall

much elaborated. It is more likely that his small craft was weighed down with a heavy object such as a quern or a piece of millstone to stabilize it.

In today's Christian calendar St Piran is remembered on 5 March. His name is perpetuated in a number of place-names in this area of Cornwall – Perranporth (St Piran's port), Perranchurch, Perranworthal, Perranzabuloe, to name but a few.

The story surrounding St Piran's Chapel or oratory is fascinating. Today it is known as 'the lost chapel of St Piran'. Until medieval times it was a well-established place of pilgrimage, visited by many people. During some violent sandstorms it was completely submerged and vanished entirely for many years.

In the late 1800s a team of archaeologists set out to discover whether the chapel really did exist. Searching beneath the sand dunes, the chapel was uncovered and documented by them. Unfortunately, due to its precarious siting, it was not possible to keep the chapel visible for long and the sand soon took over once again, filling the site.

Today the chapel still lies beneath the sand and its position is marked by a concrete slab (which at times is also in danger of being covered by a fine layer of sand).

St Piran's Cross would have provided a fine visual marker for the early pilgrims on their way to the chapel. The cross is carved from a single block of Cornish granite and, due to the extreme hardness of this stone, has no ornamentation on it. However, its fine proportions and bearing, along with the holes carved in the disc-shaped head, give it a dignity and mystique which is unique.

Since pre-Roman times, Cornwall was the largest tin-producing region in the western world. Mining tin ore from deep pits or from underground tunnels was a very hazardous occupation and from early medieval times St Piran was adopted by the 'tinners' as their patron saint. To call on his name before entering a mine shaft was said to invoke his protection.

CELTIC CHRISTIANITY

The belief systems incorporated within the early Celtic Church are today seen as an inspired progression from the dogmatic 'Churchianity' which has been prevalent for several hundred years. The Celtic affinity with nature in all her aspects, along with respect for the seasonal festivals, equality of the sexes and other important issues, is bringing new light into a declining system.

Centres such as the Iona Community, established by the late Dr George MacLeod, who was one of the pioneers of Celtic Christian awareness, are now thriving and attract more and more members, associates and friends worldwide every year.

To find out more about Celtic Christianity we have this account of its beginnings in Wales by Michael Howard, a writer and researcher on the subject who lives in Dyfed:[17]

Iona Abbey, home of the Iona Community today

It is difficult to establish the extent to which early Christianity infiltrated Roman Britain and especially Wales. Suetonius Paulinus raided Ynys Mon (Anglesey) in AD 61 in an attempt to break the political power of the Welsh druids, but it was not until AD 74 that the Roman legions conquered the Silures tribe in south Wales. A year later Roman troops occupied north Wales. Although it seems likely that the earliest Christians were members of the Roman military and civil service, apocryphal legends claim Christianity was established in Britain as early as AD 35 by the great-uncle of Jesus, Joseph of Arimathea. This rich merchant allegedly arrived in the West Country by boat from Palestine, via southern France and Brittany, and was given land at Glastonbury in Somerset by a Celtic king. On this land he established a Christian settlement and built a mud-and-wattle church dedicated to the Virgin Mary. Joseph is also supposed to have brought the Holy Grail – in Christian mythology the cup used by Jesus at the Last Supper – and to have buried it in the Glastonbury area. His visit established the first native British church and it is from these early Christian origins that Celtic Christianity was later to claim descent.

In fact, the earliest traces of the unique version of Christian belief which is today called Celtic Christianity are found at the end of the fourth century AD when the last governor of Wales, a Hispanic soldier called Magnus Maximus, was proclaimed emperor by the British legions. His Welsh wife, Elen or Helen, had been converted to Christianity after meeting St Martin of Tours in Gaul (France). When her husband was killed attempting to enforce his rule on the Roman

Empire in AD 388, Elen and her sons returned to Wales, where they established a series of Christian communities based on the monastic tradition introduced into Gaul from the Middle East by St Martin. With the end of the Roman occupation, Wales entered a period of political instability marked by internal tribal warfare, Irish invasions and outbreaks of the plague. As a result many Welsh Celts fled the country, joining with others from Ireland and Cornwall to establish a new Celtic colony in Brittany. Several of the Christian missionaries who later returned to Wales to preach the gospel and who attained the status of saints were of Breton descent.

Celtic cross design (by Anthony Rees)

At the beginning of the fifth century AD Saxon mercenaries began to arrive in south-east England to help the Romano-British nobles seize power from the demoralized remnants of the Roman legions and to help halt the incursions by the Irish and the Picts. Eventually large numbers of Saxons, Angles and Jutes from northern Germany, the Netherlands, Jutland and south Denmark settled in this country, creating Anglo-Saxon England and forcing the Celtic tribes back into Wales, Cumbria and Cornwall – all to become strongholds of Celtic Christianity.

Missionaries from Ireland, Gaul and Brittany also began to arrive in Wales and to establish religious settlements, practising what later became identified as Celtic Christianity. The followers of the new religion seem to have easily converted the ruling clases, and Christianity was imposed from above on the ordinary people, who still practised various forms of paganism, but not without a struggle. Many druids were converted, and in ancient times every Celtic tribe had a druid or shaman attached to their court who acted as a counsellor and adviser on both spiritual and secular matters. After the rulers were converted, this role was taken by a Christian priest, and many of these were former druids. Several of the famous Celtic saints were either descended from the Welsh royal families or patronized and supported by the ruling aristocracy.

Celtic Christianity differed in many ways from the Roman Church, and after the arrival of Augustine in AD 597 on his papal mission to convert the pagan Saxons, these differences were to cause serious friction. They were eventually resolved at the famous Council or Synod of Whitby in AD 664 but this led to the eventual suppression of Celtic Christianity as 'heretical', although elements of it survived in Wales as late as the Anglo-Welsh war between Prince Llewellyn and Edward 1 in the 1300s.

The Celtic Church drew its inspiration from St John and not St Paul; followed orthodox Jewish traditions dating back to the original Nazarenes; encouraged active participation by the congregation; honoured women (which was a continuance from earlier pagan Celtic spirituality); and kept the date of Easter to coincide with the Jewish Passover. Celtic bishops wore crowns, not mitres, and shaved their heads in a special style popularly known as 'the druidic tonsure'. There was also a strong monastic and hermit tradition in the Celtic Church, inherited from St Martin of Tours, influenced by the Coptic and Eastern Orthodox Churches and modelled on the ascetic practices of the early desert hermits of the Middle East.

The early Celtic Church in Wales was divided into three main groupings: bishops, who were the founding saints, such as David, Teilo, Samson, etc.; holy men, such as the saints Illtyd and Cadog, who were spiritual teachers in charge of monastic centres; and the hermits, who were wandering or pilgrim saints. They travelled across the country and between Ireland, Cornwall and Brittany, preaching the Gospel to the pagan Celtic tribes. Their solitary life of prayer, contemplation, meditation and vigil, combined with the vestiges of the old Celtic paganism, created the native mysticism and pantheistic beliefs often associated with the Celtic saints, and later with the Grail legends.

The sixth century AD was, of course, the Arthurian Age, and many of the Celtic saints and their legends are linked with the 'once and future king'. Non, mother of St David, is said to have been a pagan princess who was the niece of King Arthur, and the saint's birthplace was prophesied by Merlin. St Collen, who allegedly banished the Celtic god of the underworld, Gwynn ap Nudd, from his home on Glastonbury Tor, the entrance to the Otherworld in Celtic mythology, was said to have been one of the warriors of the Round Table Fellowship. St Dyfrig presided over the coronation of the young Arthur at Caerleon, while St Illtyd, who was originally a druid, is described in some legends as 'the guardian of the Grail'. Such connections between the Celtic saints, the Arthurian myths, Glastonbury as a pagan and early Christian centre and the Grail myths are highly significant.

By the beginning of the fourteenth century, the Celtic Church was effectively a spent force in Wales, yet in the Tudor period there was a brief revival of interest in the native British Church when Matthew Parker, chaplain to Queen Anne Boleyn and the second Protestant archbishop of Canterbury, ordered Welsh monks to research the Joseph of Arimathea story and the legend of the sixth-century bard Taliesin. The aim of this investigation was to provide historical proof that Christianity existed in Britain before the arrival of Augustine and his Roman missionaries, which could be used to counteract Rome's objection to the English Reformation.

In recent times there have been several serious works published on the subject that have attempted to show its relevance to modern society because of Celtic Christianity's unique approach to the natural world.

Celtic cross design (by Anthony Rees)

The ancient heritage of Celtic Christianity makes it relevant for today because orthodox Churchianity has rejected the sacredness of the natural world, the concept that God (or whatever we call the Divine Source) could be contacted through nature and feminine spirituality. All these were important aspects of the pre-Christian world view. The rejection of these aspects has had a detrimental effect on human society over the last 1500 years and we are only just realizing the damage this has caused to both the collective psyche of the human race and the planetary environment. At a time when the modern Church is in crisis, Celtic Christianity may well be a milestone in the creation of an enlightened Christianity for the twenty-first century.

To carry this chapter on Celtic Christianity into the present tense, there follows an account by Peter Glanville, a modern-day pilgrim, of a visit to the Iona Community, along with reflections on the Celtic way of life.

The Iona Community was built on the site of St Columba's original monastery and now, over 1400 years later, is one of the main centres for the re-emergence of Celtic Christianity in today's world.

I have been interested in Celtic culture and spirituality for some time. A few hours spent on Iona in 1993, followed by nearly a week's stay in the abbey, gave me firsthand experience of communal life 'Celtic style' as it were. St Columba founded a monastic settlement here in the sixth century AD. Celtic monasticism and church life in general were somewhat different to their Roman counterparts. The Celtic way was less structured. The parochial system was conceived by the Roman Church, while the Celtic Church was composed of *ad hoc* communities evolving from the tribal system of pre-Christian times.

Celtic Christianity was able to build on much raw material already in existence. It did not seek to stamp out an ancient culture which in

The Abbey Church of St Mary, with St Oran's Chapel in the foreground, Iona

many ways valued the sacred as a part of everyday life. The brand of Christianity which St Columba spread was gentle and all-embracing. It absorbed those aspects of paganism which were seen to be beneficial. Popular belief has it that St Columba was on friendly terms with one of the druids. He is also reputed to have referred to Jesus as his druid.

In the Celtic scheme of the universe there is little, if any, veil between this world and the next. Celtic Christians, like their pagan predecessors, often claimed to be in touch with other dimensions. For the pagan peoples nature spirits were a reality, and for the early Celtic Christians Jesus, the Virgin Mary and Brigit, a pre-Christian goddess who was 'Christianized' to become St Bride, also had enormous influence on their lives. The sacred and the secular worlds were not seen as being in opposition to each other, but rather as part of the whole.

Dr George MacLeod founded the Iona Community on the site of the Benedictine abbey which was built in the Middle Ages over the foundations of the original sixth-century Celtic monastic settlement of Columcille or St Columba. The ruins of the abbey buildings were rebuilt under the supervision of this pioneering minister in the 1930s, and it is now a major centre for promoting peace and spiritual studies. Many of the strands of Celtic spirituality are woven into the liturgy. The music, which plays an important part in the life of the community, is distinctly Celtic in flavour. The Celtic approach to spirituality is very much in tune with contemporary thinking, and concern for environmental issues and the greening of the planet is one example. Linked to this is the sacredness of matter and the spiritualizing of all things material. Dr MacLeod used these words: 'The spiritual and the material are one, and are divided by the abstraction of thought.' The French palaeontologist, priest and mystic Teilhard de Chardin incorporated much which could be traced back to the Celtic reverence for life in his writings. A number of leading members of the scientific community, including Fritjof Capra for example, are stressing the interconnectedness of everything in the universe. Matthew Fox, the Catholic priest, writer and educator, with his promotion of Creation Spirituality, the mysticism of Hildegard of Bingen, St Julian of Norwich, Meister Eckhardt and others also incorporate the Celtic vision within their teachings.

For myself, I am indebted to two contemporary authors on Celtic Christianity with whom I have had conversations.[18] Their considerable knowledge of the subject has enabled me gradually to understand the complexities of Celtic history, and also the essential vision of hope which is permeating different levels of society.

The Iona Community embodies this spirit of hope, and the tiny sacred Hebridean island receives many thousands of pilgrims from all over the world each year.

To conclude this chapter on Celtic Christianity here is Mada James's account of a pilgrimage to Lindisfarne or Holy Island, located just off the Northumbrian coast, not far from Berwick-upon-Tweed. This was another flourishing island-based Celtic monastic community, initiated in the seventh century AD by St Aidan. The exquisite illuminated Gospels which bear its name is legendary.

There must be few places more redolent of Celtic spirituality than
Lindisfarne, the Holy Isle. Here life is reduced to its ultimate elements
– earth and air and sea, man and nature, matter and spirit – and all
interwoven by the presence of God. And it is Aidan, an Irish Celt
trained as a monk on Iona, who is at the heart of it all.

In the seventh century AD a prince who had spent his youth on
Iona became king of Northumbria, and decided that this realm of wild
and savage fighting tribes needed the influence of the Christian
teaching which he had had. The first group of monks sent at his
request from Iona returned in despair and disgust – nothing could ever
be done with these wicked barbarians! But because Aidan thought
otherwise, he was sent forth with a few companions to try again.

King Oswald had perhaps already known him on Iona; at any rate,
he gave his warm support and friendship, acted as his interpreter (for

Aidan was totally ignorant of the Northumbrian language at first) and offered him the land of his choice as a base. Thus he and his group settled on Lindisfarne and there built up their little community.

What place could be more fitting? For half the day it is an island where, uninterrupted, the monks could pray and work and worship together. When the tide ebbs, it is linked to the mainland, so they could go forth and teach the local people and be visited by any who wished to come. They lived like ordinary people of the area, in simplicity and near povery, worshipping in a primitive little chapel and living in simple huts. The great Benedictine priory, the remains of which can be seen on the island today, was built at a later date. (In 1082 Lindisfarne was linked with the monastic establishment at Durham, and Lindisfarne Priory was nearing completion by the year 1100.)

Though Aidan was soon appointed Bishop of Northumbria, he saw himself as shepherd of a flock rather than a prince of the Church, walking everywhere (when presented with a splendid horse by a royal patron, he gave it to a poor farmer who needed one), talking to all he met, teaching and making friends. He set up a school for local boys, some of whom were slaves whom he had bought with any money given to him. He later encouraged Hilda of Whitby, a nun, to do the same for girls.

So this man, coming as a foreigner, speaking a different language and preaching an alien religion, became accepted and loved by the wild Northumbrians. He and his monks taught, and showed by the way they lived their lives, that love, gentleness and mercy were greater weapons than hate and violence, and to suffer for one's faith

The ruins of Lindisfarne Priory

was as heroic as to fight. And their Christianity was imbued with the Celtic tradition, which brought God and the saints into every sphere of living, so that dressing, milking the cow, rowing a boat, all became part of prayer and praise. So Christianity, interwoven with all that was best in the earlier belief systems, spread over the region and beyond, and many monasteries were founded. With the support of King Oswald and his successor Oswy, Aidan laid down the foundations for a centre of spirituality, art and learning which was to become the greatest of its age in Britain.

Not many remarkable stories survive about Aidan, as they do about his successor St Cuthbert; two or three miraculous happenings and healings, and a few sayings. We know only that he lived simply, won the affection of many and withdrew at times to that island in the Inner Farnes (page 109), which we associate with St Cuthbert, for solitary meditation. St Cuthbert himself, when Abbot of Lindisfarne, spent no less than nine of his 16 years as a hermit on this tiny island, which is named after him.

We know of the monasteries that Aidan founded, and that the boys in his school, as well as the monks, read and understood Latin, and learned how to copy and illuminate their own manuscripts. The historian Bede wrote admiringly that Aidan and his monks 'lived as they taught', and that those trained in his tradition later carried the Christian message far beyond the borders of Northumbria, as far south as the Midlands.

He died on Lindisfarne and was buried there. A contemporary statue commemorates him but there is no shrine like St Cuthbert's in Durham Cathedral. But surely the Holy Isle is his memorial, along with his spirit, which tangibly permeates the atmosphere on the island. In addition, there is the Celtic sense of the intricate interweaving of sea and rocks and sky, man and beast and bird and God, in a pattern as subtle and beautiful as those which would later adorn the pages of the Lindisfarne Gospels.

Contemporary statue of St Aidan, Lindisfarne, with the ruins of the twelfth-century priory to the right. Lindisfarne Castle can be seen on the horizon to the right of St Aidan

THE ILLUMINATED GOSPELS

To many people the essence of Celtic Christianity is embodied in the early illuminated Gospels. In describing them, superlatives are inadequate and many regard the major examples, the Books of Kells and Lindisfarne as some of the finest artwork the world has ever seen.

Their exquisite and elaborate detail profoundly affected a travelling ecclesiastic, Giraldus Cambrensis (Gerald of Wales), in the late 1100s while he was journeying through Ireland, visiting *en route* a monastery at Kildare. Translations of his diaries of travels through Wales, and a few years later through Ireland, are still available today.

In the account of his travels through Ireland,[19] after seeing one of the illuminated Gospels, he writes:

> If you take the trouble to look very closely, and penetrate with your eyes to the secrets of the artistry, you will notice such intricacies, so delicate and subtle, so close together and well knitted, so involved and bound together, and so fresh in their colourings that you will not hesitate to declare that all of these things must have been the work, not of men, but of angels.

St Cuthbert's Island, off Lindisfarne, with the ruins of the early chapel and cross visible

There are many people who would echo these sentiments today.

These Gospels were the products of Celtic monks whose artwork was wholly dedicated to the beauty of creation. There are various well-illustrated specialist books on the Gospels,[20] so we will concern ourselves here with only outline descriptions of the three finest, the illuminated Gospel Books of Kells, Lindisfarne and Durrow.

Unlike today, time was not an important factor in the lives of the early Celtic monks, so the many months or even years that it took to produce these exquisite works of art would have been creatively rewarding and fulfilling for the artist or artists involved.

The best-known of the illuminated Gospels is the Book of Kells, although a number of smaller, lesser-known manuscripts of a similar style, mostly of a slightly later date, were produced in Ireland, Britain and subsequently Europe by travelling Irish monks or their descendants.

The magnificent Book of Kells takes its name from the early Irish monastery of this name in County Meath, Ireland. Today the high cross of the monastery is still standing, rather eroded by over a thousand years of exposure to the Irish weather, yet details of the highly intricate carvings can still be seen on both the cross and the base in which it is set.

Tradition has it that the Book of Kells was originally created on the island of Iona and, during one of the frequent Viking invasions of the island, was taken for safekeeping to Ireland and kept at the monastery of Kells. The first actual reference to it is an entry in the *Annals of Ulster,* for 1006, where it is recorded as having been stolen from the church at Kells and found 'after 20 nights and two months, its gold having been stolen off it, and a sod over it'.

The manuscript itself is one of the great wonders of the Celtic world in its beauty and complexity. It dates from the late eighth century AD and uses many brightly coloured natural pigments, blue, green, yellow and red-brown being the predominant colours. The blue was made from powdered lapis lazuli, which would certainly have been brought from the Continent, as there are no known sources of this mineral in the British Isles.

The ornament of the Book of Kells is profuse and very varied, incorporating Pictish, Anglo-Saxon and Byzantine influences, as well as indigenous Celtic themes. The three main constructional elements of Celtic art – spirals, knotwork and key-patterning – are found here at their best and most elaborate, and the scale of many of the units is minute. As an example, on the 'chi-rho monogram' page there is a panel containing four monks pulling each other's beards, surrounded by interlacing. The panel is rectangular and the length of the longest side is just 2.2 centimetres (9/10 in)! Though it is known that a grid system was used to form the basis for the main outlines and knotwork, it is still a matter of speculation as to how these motifs were drawn on such a small scale. Today it would require a powerful magnifying glass to paint, say, several bird or plant motifs surrounded by complex knotwork within the space of two square centimetres of vellum, as does frequently occur. Over the centuries a number of eminent figures have described the Book of Kells as one of the finest works of art in the whole world.

The high cross at Kells, County Meath

The contemporary painting shown on page 112 incorporates designs from the Book of Kells.

During the Cromwellian period the Book of Kells was presented to Trinity College, Dublin, most probably by Henry Jones, Bishop of Meath from 1661 to 1682. To this day it can still be admired under glass in the library there, about 1200 years after its creation by Celtic monks.

For the enthusiast, there is a fine facsimile reproduction version available depicting all the illuminated pages, with an introductory text.[21]

Next we have a description of the magnificent Lindisfarne Gospels, and the island on which the book was created. It was fashioned by Celtic monks of Irish descent on the Holy Island of Lindisfarne, after they had settled there from Iona in the seventh century AD.

The island of Lindisfarne, after which the magnificent Gospels are named, lies about three kilometres (one and a half miles) off the coast of Northumbria, separated by a causeway accessible only at low tide. Today one can make a pilgrimage to the ruins of Lindisfarne Priory, built between 1083 and 1100 as a dependency of Durham Cathedral, on the site of the original monastery.

The original Celtic settlement on Lindisfarne was founded by St Aidan in *c.* AD 635. The Gospels were written and illuminated here about half a century later, probably between AD 687 and 698.

That the Gospels are very closely related to the Book of Kells there can be no doubt, bearing, as they do, the distinctive style of the Irish Celtic artists. The earliest historic references to the Gospels' origins are in the manuscript itself. In the tenth century AD, 250 years after it had been created, a priest called Aldred added an Anglo-Saxon translation of the Latin text, and on the last page he wrote the following:

Eadfrith, Bishop of the Lindisfarne Church, originally wrote this book, for God and Saint Cuthbert and, jointly, for all the Saints whose relics are in the island. And Ethelwald, Bishop of the Lindisfarne islanders, impressed it on the outside and covered it, as he well knew how. And Billfrith the anchorite forged the ornaments which are on it on the outside and adorned it with gold and gems and with gilded-over silver, pure metal. And Aldred, unworthy and most miserable priest, glossed it in English between the lines with the help of God and Saint Cuthbert.

Contemporary painting incorporating many different designs from the Book of Kells (by Simon Rouse)

The 'carpet page' from the Book of Lindisfarne

The link with Ireland and the Irish tradition of the great illuminated Gospels can be traced to the lovely island of Iona, off the west coast of Scotland. King Oswald of Northumbria, eager to establish Celtic Christianity in his realm, sent a request to Iona for Irish priests to establish themselves on Lindisfarne. A group of missionaries, led by St Aidan, came from Iona and founded the monastery on Holy Island. St Cuthbert, to whom the Gospels are dedicated, was St Aidan's successor. The Book of Kells was almost certainly created on Iona by Celtic monks who had travelled there from Ireland, so the knowledge of manuscript illumination would have been carried to Northumbria by St Aidan and his followers.

The Gospels themselves are almost as magnificent as the Book of Kells, and are another jewel of the Celtic Christian world. Again, the size of the individual panels is minute, and some form of magnification must surely have been used to execute them. The main pages are of exquisite elaborateness, employing highly evolved spirals, knotwork and key-patterning. Interestingly, the only stylistic difference from the Book of Kells is one particular bird form, found only in the Book of Lindisfarne.

At the end of the eighth century AD Lindisfarne, like other holy islands including Iona, was invaded and pillaged by the Vikings. Fortunately, the Great Gospel survived, and several years later was taken, along with the reliquary containing the relics of St Cuthbert, to the mainland for safekeeping. For a while it remained at Chester-le-Street, County Durham, which was where the priest Aldred added his Anglo-Saxon postscript.

Soon after this the Gospels were taken to Durham Cathedral with the relics of St Cuthbert. They then faded into obscurity for a while, reappearing in 1567, when the first dictionary of the Anglo-Saxon language, the *Vocabulum Saxonicum* was produced, using Aldred's Latin/Anglo-Saxon translation in the Gospels for its guide. At this time it is said that the Gospels were kept in the Tower Jewel House, London, on account of their lavish gold and jewelled binding.

In the early 1600s they were bought by Sir Robert Cotton, possessor of a magnificent library of ancient manuscripts. After his death, his heirs made the collection over to the nation in 1703, and in 1753 it was

Contemporary painting incorporating many different designs from the Book of Lindisfarne (by Simon Rouse)

incorporated into the British Museum as one of its main features and can still be seen there to this day.

The state of the binding when it was presented to the British Museum was very poor, and in 1852 a London firm of craft-jewellers rebound them using silver and precious stones. The beautiful designs for this cover were all taken from the original eighth-century manuscript.

The Lindisfarne Gospels are one of the treasures of the Celtic Christian world, and for those fascinated by the Celtic art form they deserve detailed study.

The contemporary painting shown on page 114 incorporates designs from the Lindisfarne Gospels.

The last illuminated Gospel book that we will look at is the Book of Durrow. This is the earliest surviving illuminated Gospel and dates from around AD 675. Today it rests safely in Trinity College library, Dublin, along with the Book of Kells.

The manuscript illumination of the Book of Durrow has a basic 'earthiness' about its artwork which serves to enhance rather than detract from its beauty. Red ochre, yellow ochre, olive-green and black are the predominant colours, though other colours are employed sparingly.

It has 248 pages and is profusely decorated. There are six majestic 'carpet pages' filled entirely with Celtic ornamentation. The overall size of each page is 24.5 by 14 centimetres (ten by five and a half in).

The detail and accuracy of the knotwork and spiral decoration are truly magnificent, especially on the 'carpet pages'. In many of the knot-work borders clever use is made of an optical illusion effect with three different colours in sequence which adds shape and depth to what would otherwise be a comparitively plain design (as much as any design in the Book of Durrow can be called plain!).

The symbols of the Four Evangelists are very stark and basic, yet retain a sense of great power and beauty. Man, the symbol of St Matthew, with his very strong outline and highly chequered coat, has been given the rather undignified name of a 'walking buckle' by some less appreciative historians. The spiral ornament in the Gospels is of the finest detail and accuracy, and the artists who created this masterpiece were highly experienced with this art form.

The Gospel's place of creation is not known. It takes its name from the monastery in County Meath, Ireland, which was founded by St Columba. On the last page of the Gospels there is a later inscription testifying that it was present in Durrow monastery around the turn of the twelfth century.

Three possibilities are put forward as to its place of creation. The first is Durrow itself, which would seem quite likely as the designs in the Gospel bear much similarity to Irish metalwork of the same era. The second is Iona, which is also quite feasible, as the island was inhabited by Irish monks from the time of St Columba, and is also known to have had a massive library which was pillaged by the Vikings. Fleeing monks may well have removed the major Gospel works to safer environments, as is thought to have happened with the Book of Kells. The third possibility is that it was created on the island of Lindisfarne. Lindisfarne had a very strong Irish monastic connection at that time.

Irrespective of its place of origin, this, the earliest and one of the finest great illuminated Gospel books, has survived for over 1300 years to find sanctuary in Trinity College, Dublin, where it is under careful supervision.

The history of the Book of Durrow after the twelfth century is virtually unknown. For the admirer of exquisite Celtic art, however, it is wonderful to know that these three major illuminated Gospel books of Kells, Lindisfarne and Durrow have survived the ravages of time and can still be viewed with awe and wonder today.

Many readers will have encountered the Books of Kells and Lindisfarne, but it is less well known that there was a subsequent radiation of Celtic art via travelling Irish monks or their descendants to many different countries. Surprisingly, a number of these manuscripts, which were either taken abroad by the monks or created overseas by them and their students, still exist in museums worldwide. It might come as a surprise to learn that St Petersburg in Russia is home to the Leningrad Gospels, a very fine late eighth-century Northumbrian-Celtic illuminated manuscript. It can be seen in St Petersburg Public Library, where there is another Celtic illuminated manuscript, a copy of Bede's *Ecclesiastical History*, dating from AD 746. It is thought that both these manuscripts arrived in St Petersburg at a later date, and may well have been given as royal gifts.

A number of other Celtic illuminated manuscripts, or parts of them, still exist. Examples are the eighth-century Gospels of MacRegol, which can be found in the Bodleian Library, Oxford, while the ninth-century Book of Armagh is in the Royal Irish Academy in Dublin. The tenth-century Gospels of MacDurnan are in Lambeth Library, London.

Soon after the era of the Lindisfarne Gospels, illuminated manuscripts were being created in the south of England by Celtic monks and their students. These include the Canterbury Bible, the Vespasian Psalter and the Book of Cerne, all containing pages with knotwork, spirals and key-patterning.

The monastic settlement at Tours in France, patronized by Charlemagne, produced some finely illuminated Gospels with strong Northumbrian-Celtic influence *c.* AD 800. Two of these, the Bible of Charles the Bald and the St Martin-des-Champs Gospels are in the National Library of Paris. Both these manuscripts have striking artistic links with the Books of Kells and Lindisfarne. Likewise the Gospels of Echternach and Maaseik, and the Trier Gospels of the mid-eighth century, have fine illuminated pages of Celtic-influenced artwork.

Other volumes are the Gospels of Cutbercht, now in Vienna National Library, and the Barberini Gospels in the Vatican Library, Rome. There is also the Montpelier Psalter, now in Montpelier University Library.

These examples help to give some idea of the spread of the Celtic art form, from its roots in Ireland, western Scotland and Northumbria to various parts of Europe, and indeed eventually as far afield as Russia. This is universal beauty indeed, still admired and revered today as being some of the finest artwork ever produced.

CONTINUING THE TRADITION

Today there is a great resurgence of the Celtic spirit. Communities and centres which base their lifestyles around the Celts of Iron Age Britain and Europe, and also those which embrace Celtic Christianity, are flourishing.

For one thing, Celtic music abounds in the folk and folk-rock circuits of the UK, Europe, North America and Australasia. The resurgence of the music via festivals, tours and the availability of CDs has definitely helped – from pure unaccompanied Gaelic to the loudness of Runrig. But that's not all.

Craftworkers in many and varied media are employing Celtic designs and much beautiful work is being produced. The best, as with any creative art or craftwork, embodies new and exciting designs, taking as a foundation the early art forms and producing creations which are fresh and alive.

Nowadays there are Celtic craftworkers producing all types of jewellery, from gold and silver to bronze, copper and pewter, and also leatherwork, original artwork printed as books, cards, posters, T-shirts and stationery, stained glass, pottery, resin-casting, carvings in stone and wood, as well as craftwork in various other media.

Many of these crafts have enjoyed a renaissance in the twentieth century, and some employ materials which were not available to the original Celts. Just a few skills have continued in an unbroken tradition from their early beginnings, and we include two unusual and beautiful ones here.

Mike Davies at work in his studio and gallery; notice examples of his exquisite work hanging top left

The first is the art of Welsh lovespoon carving, and the description of the craft and its history is by Mike Davies, a Welsh master-carver, whose creations have found their way into museums and collections worldwide.[22]

The delightful custom of giving lovespoons (*llwyau caru* in Welsh) began in Wales as early as the sixteenth century, although the earliest dated example is a spoon of 1667 which forms part of the collection of the Welsh Folk Museum at St Fagans, near Cardiff.

The art of making elaborately carved spoons was a natural extension of domestic spoon-carving. In particular the cawl, or soup spoon, which in the fifteenth and sixteenth centuries would have been made on quite a regular basis in most country households.

Being a woodcarver of spoons myself, I can easily visualize the country folk sitting around large open fires on winter evenings, a young man carving away at the manufacture of domestic spoons, his thoughts turning to love. He would then decorate the handle of the spoon with a message of love: maybe the initials of a pretty young girl in his village carved alongside his own. He would spend many hours carving and polishing the spoon prior to presenting it to the girl, with the hope that this gift of love would begin a lifelong relationship.

The term 'spooning', meaning courting behaviour, is a romantic illustration of the connection between love and a spoon. It is natural that the term used about courting couples arose from the making and giving of lovespoons.

Many of the young spoon-carvers would by day have worked on the land, or have been attached to a large country house or estate where there would have been quite a variety of very skilled craftsmen employed, including builders, artists, woodcarvers, leatherworkers, wheelwrights and blacksmiths. It was from these artists and craftsmen that the development of the many symbols and forms of decoration began.

Over the years there was a gradual elaboration of this simple utensil – the handles were extended and widened, and an endless variety of symbols were carved into them to express the maker's feelings for his young lady; and because more than one beau may have competed for the favours of the same local beauty, it was often important to include in the design some form of identification. This was frequently achieved by using symbols which related to the carver's profession or personal interests.

Possibly a sailor would carve a ship or an anchor, a farmer might use an animal or corn, a stable lad a horse, or maybe just an initial or names and dates would have been employed.

Not all suitors were able to carve their own spoons, so they often employed the services of a local woodcarver to make a spoon for them, using the appropriate and agreed symbols.

The custom has continued from these early origins to the present day. The lovespoon still makes a charming gift to a loved one, and can be made to depict any expression of love. They may be given nowadays to simply say 'I love you', or to commemorate births, christenings, birthdays, engagements, weddings, anniversaries and other special occasions.

These days both public and private collectors the world over are

One of Mike Davies's lovespoons, with traditional knotwork patterning from the Book of Kells

including high-quality Welsh lovespoons in their collections. I have been fortunate to carve lovespoons for many illustrious people, including HM The Queen Mother and ex-President Gorbachev of Russia. It would seem that discerning collectors are seeking out lovespoons produced by one of the handful of carvers who make them with the same feeling, understanding and love for the wood and work that their ancestors had in times gone by.

During the past few years it has been a special delight for me to exhibit and demonstrate my craft at the Wesh Folk Museum in Cardiff on a regular basis. I have also demonstrated my craft on an HTV series *The Makers*, filmed at St Fagans with TV presenter Jan Leeming.

Nowadays I have a student and assistant who has a fine natural ability with wood and is dedicated to continuing this rare and beautiful tradition of craftsmanship.

Next we look at a very ancient craft, that of harp-making. The Irish harp and its music has a legendary place in the Celtic sagas and myths, as well as being represented historically in early Celtic stone carvings dating from the 8th and 9th century both in Ireland and western Scotland. It is an interesting fact that the BBC television 'Time Team' archaeologists recently discovered metal harp tuning-pegs when excavating the site of the Lords of The Isles at Finlaggan, on the Isle of Islay, western Scotland.

Our account of the history of the Irish harp is by George Stevens, a fine harp-maker and historian living in Cornwall (an illustration of his harps is shown on page 118):[23]

I first visited Ireland in the late 1970s, since when my interest in the country, its people, culture, turbulent political and social history, and primarily its music, has steadily grown. Most of the Irish traditional music played today originated in the seventeenth and eighteenth centuries, but the Irish harping tradition is far more ancient. These factors, along with the inspirational Queen Mary harp preserved in Edinburgh's National Museum of Antiquities, have formed the basis of my work as a maker and researcher of early instruments.

Research into this subject can be divided into three areas. The first is pictorial evidence. Evidence of the earliest harps known to the Gaelic peoples is left to us on Celtic and Pictish stones of around the eighth and ninth centuries, towards the end of the Dark Age period from which very little literature survives. Pictish stones in eastern Scotland depicting the harp have been found from Aldbar, Dupplin, Nigg and Monifieth, while in western Scotland there are examples in Iona Cathedral and St Oran's Chapel on Iona.

The second area of research is historiography. Statements by contemporary observers are available from around the twelfth century, although until the eighteenth and nineteenth centuries they come primarily from foreigners. Outside the Irish monasteries the majority of the population was illiterate, and even among the literate the teaching of harping was conveyed orally and in secret. The nineteenth century saw a renewed interest in the Irish harp, ironically during a period when the instrument in its original form was no longer in use.

The third area of research is the instruments themselves. There are only 14 surviving instruments and fragments representing the entire known period of use of the traditional form of the Irish harp, a sad remnant of what must once have been an army of thousands. Unfortunately the harp makers were not in the habit of signing and dating their instruments. Only a small minority of the extant examples bear names and/or dates, thus making accurate dating rather difficult.

The harps on the early Pictish stones are shown as being constructed with two main parts, the sound-box and the string bar or harmonic curve, and sometimes with a third part, the forepillar, whose addition introduced greater stability and must surely have facilitated a far wider range of tuning possibilities and increased the sonority of the instruments by allowing greater string tension. However, if the dating of these stone carvings is accurate, it would appear that both forms coexisted for several centuries.

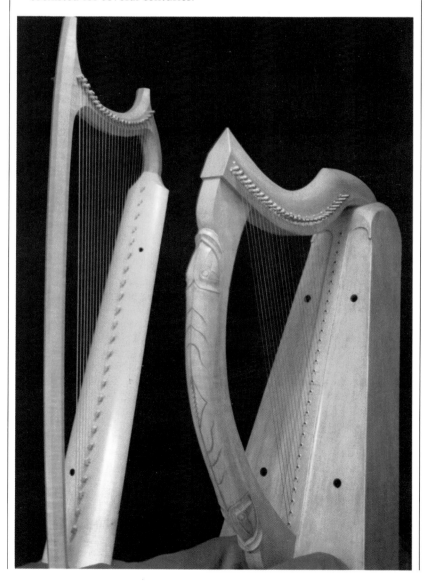

Reproduction Gothic (left) and Irish (right) harps (by George Stevens)

The Irish took the process one stage further, creating an instrument of bulky, robust and essentially much heavier construction than any other throughout the numerous countries in which harps were esteemed. The reason was surely to enable the harps to withstand the considerable tension exerted by the thick brass strings on which the Irish loved to play, a practice unique to any form of harp from any period. This change had taken place certainly by the fourteenth century (a fine example is preserved in Trinity College, Dublin) but may have occurred much earlier. Brass strung harps were being used in Ireland by the twelfth century, according to Giraldus Cambrensis (see page 109), though unfortunately for us he gives no indication of the form of the instruments used.

By the fourteenth century European harps can be divided into two recognizable forms: the heavily built Irish harp and the much more delicate instrument commonly referred to as the Gothic or Romanesque harp. While the latter was superseded by other forms, the Irish harp was to remain essentially the same in concept for approximately another three and a half centuries. The view of much of today's general public is that any harp other than the large orchestral instrument is called an Irish harp. They are normally referring to instruments made by the nineteenth-century Dublin maker John Egan. Yes, Egan was a Dubliner, therefore the harps were Irish; however, the resemblance to their predecessors is minimal. The Egan harps had a much lighter construction and were clearly inspired more by the pedal harps of his day than by the true Irish harp which forms the subject of this treatise.

The history and emergence of the Irish harp in its first recognizable standardized form is very difficult to trace. Very few instruments of *any* kind survive which predate the fourteenth century; regarding harps in particular, pictorial and literary evidence is relatively scarce.

Professor Eugene O'Curry, in his extensive nineteenth-century work *The Manners and Customs of the Ancient Irish*, attributes the possible origin of the Irish harp to Greece, finding its way to Ireland via the Tuatha Dé Danann, a race of people whose story, among many others, is chronicled in *The Book of Conquest and Invasions*, a very ancient book of what O'Curry calls 'traditions and writings'. The Tuatha Dé Danann inhabited the area of Greece in which Athens is situated and, following the invasion of a fleet from Syria, they were forced to flee northwards and westwards into Europe, finally settling in Ireland.

Our attention is drawn to the similarity between the Irish and Egyptian legends of how the harp was invented. The Irish legend tells of how a woman walking along the beach fell asleep after hearing the music caused by the wind blowing through the sinews of a whale skeleton that was lying nearby. The potential was realized by her husband, who went immediately and fashioned a frame from wood and furnished it with the whale sinews – this became the first *cruit* (harp). The Egyptian version goes as follows. The Nile river, having overflowed the whole country of Egypt, had left a great number of dead animals in its wake as it subsided. Mercury, walking along the riverbank, struck his foot against the shell of a tortoise whose flesh had been dried out by the sun so that all that remained were the cartilages which had been stretched and dried in the heat. The sound resulting so pleased Mercury that it suggested to him the idea for the lyre.

121

One of the ornamented compartments of a sculptured Celtic cross at the church of Ullard in County Kilkenny, Ireland, shows a seated harp player whose instrument is noticed in Edward Bunting's *Ancient Music of Ireland* of 1840 for its similarity to ancient Egyptian harps. This harp could be described as quadrangular, although it lacks a forepillar, a feature which Bunting notes is the first to be discovered outside Egypt. A date for the Ullard Cross is not specifically given, although its workmanship and style are comparable with the cross of Muiredach at Monasterboice (see page 95).

Celtic harpists Dominig Bouchaud from Brittany and Kora Wüthier from Switzerland in concert at the Celtic Days festival in Switzerland, 1995

Today the harp is taught and played widely, not only in all the Celtic countries but throughout the world. There is an annual harp festival in Japan, which gives some idea of the universal popularity of the instrument.

In Switzerland recently an annual festival called Celtic Days has been established, based around the harp and harp music, along with other aspects of Celtic culture. Switzerland is an ideal place for an annual Celtic festival as Lake Neuchâtel was the main centre of the La Tène Celtic culture from the fifth to the third centuries BC. Harpists from many countries, both professional and amateur, attend and there are workshops on making historical instruments, as well as concerts given by leading harpists from different nations. Of course, there are also the regular and by now huge Celtic festivals in Brittany, at Quimper and L'Orient, and the more recent UK festival – aptly called Celtic Connections – in Glasgow each New Year.

AFTERWORD

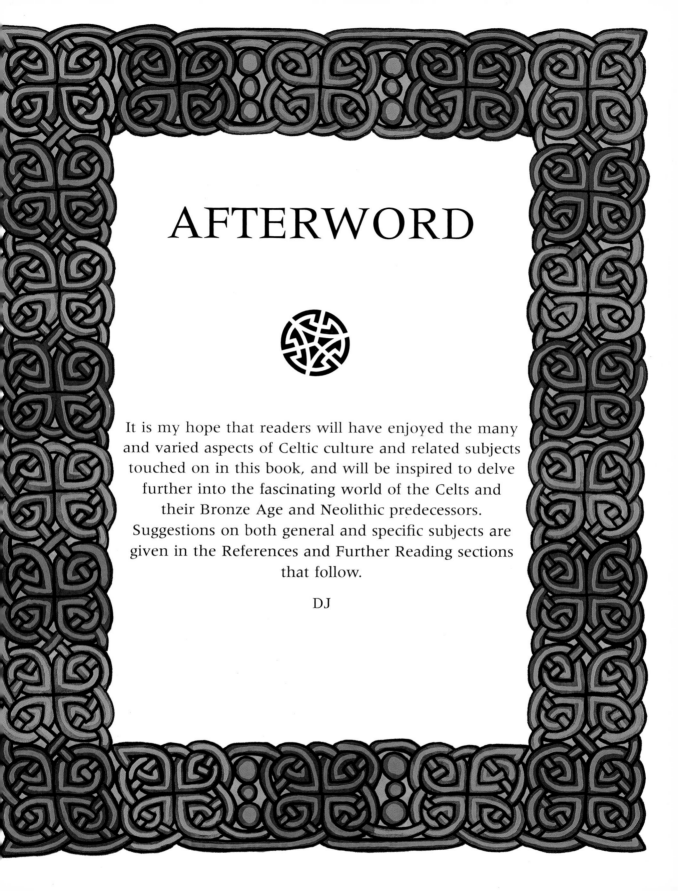

It is my hope that readers will have enjoyed the many
and varied aspects of Celtic culture and related subjects
touched on in this book, and will be inspired to delve
further into the fascinating world of the Celts and
their Bronze Age and Neolithic predecessors.
Suggestions on both general and specific subjects are
given in the References and Further Reading sections
that follow.

DJ

REFERENCES

1 *The Times Atlas of World History*, HarperCollins, 1994
2 W. Y. Evans-Wentz, *The Fairy Faith in Celtic Countries*, first published in 1911, reprinted by Colin Smythe, 1977
3 Ibid.
4 Alistair Service and Jean Bradbury, *The Standing Stones of Europe*, J. M. Dent, 1993
5 Alexander Thom, *Megalithic Lunar Observatories*, Oxford, 1973
6 Alexander and A. S. Thom, *Megalithic Remains in Britain and Brittany*, Oxford, 1979
7 Anne Ross, *Pagan Celtic Britain*, Constable & Co., 1992
8 John King, *The Celtic Druid's Year*, Blandford Press, 1994
9 Anand Chetan and Diane Brueton, *The Sacred Yew*, Arcana Press, 1994
10 Ibid.
11 David Clarke, *A Guide to Britain's Pagan Heritage*, Hale Press, 1995
12 Tim Severin, *The Brendan Voyage*, Hutchinson, 1978
13 Maureen Costain Richards, *The Manx Crosses Illuminated*, Croshag Publications, 1988, available from Ballabrara Arts, Port St Mary, Isle of Man
14 J. Romilly Allen, *Celtic Art in Pagan and Christian Times*, first published 1904, reprinted by Bracken Books, 1993
15 Isabel Henderson, 'The Art and Function of Rosmarkie's Pictish Monuments,' 1989
16 Marianna Lines, *Sacred Stones, Sacred Places: An Illustrated History of Pictish Sites*, St Andrews Press, 1993
17 Michael Howard, *Angels and Goddesses: Celtic Christianity and Paganism in Ancient Britain*, Capall Bann Publishing, 1993
18 Ian Bradley, *The Celtic Way*, Darton, Longman and Todd, 1993, and Shirley Toulson, *The Celtic Alternative: A Reminder of the Christianity We Lost*, Random Century, 1987
19 Gerald of Wales, *The History and Topography of Ireland*, translated by J. J. O'Meara, London, 1982
20 Janet Backhouse, *The Lindisfarne Gospels*, Phaidon Press, 1981, and *The Book of Kells*, described by Edward Sullivan, 1920, reprinted 1986 and 1992 by Studio Editions Ltd
21 François Henri, *The Book of Kells*, Studio Reproduction Edition, Thames & Hudson, 1974
22 *Mike Davies*, 'Welsh Lovespoons', illustrated booklet of history available from Tredegar House, Newport, Gwent NP1 9YW
23 George Stevens *The Irish Harp, Its History, Players and Techniques*, available from 31 Bar Terrace, Falmouth, Cornwall TR11 4BP

FURTHER READING

Bryce, Derek, *Symbolism of the Celtic Cross*, Llanerch Publishers, Felinfach, Dyfed, 1989, revised edition 1994

Clarke, David, *Twilight of the Celtic Gods*, Blandford, 1996

Davis, Courtney, and James, David, *The Celtic Image*, Blandford, 1996

Dixon-Kennedy, Mike, *Celtic Myth & Legend: An A–Z of People and Places*, Blandford, 1996

Laing, Lloyd, *Celtic Britain*, Routledge & Kegan Paul, 1979

Seaborne, Malcolm, *Celtic Crosses of Britain and Ireland*, Shire Publications, 1989, reprinted 1994

Straffon, Cheryl, *The Earth Goddess*, Blandford, 1997; *Pagan Cornwall, Land of the Goddess*, Meyn Mamvro Publications, 1993

Wilde, Lyn Webster, *Celtic Women – in Myth, Legend and History*, Blandford, 1996

INDEX

Page numbers in *italic* refer to illustrations